"We are created for stories. We read stories, tell stories, watch stories, and live in stories. Yet we instinctively know and long for our stories to fit into something bigger, more meaningful, and more comprehensive. As we read Scripture, we can see how that longing might be fulfilled, but we don't always know how to connect our own stories to the great story of redemption that culminates with Christ. This is why I'm so thankful for David Murray's StoryChanger series. These short devotionals are wonderful guides for connecting our stories with God's larger story and helping us call others into God's great story. I gladly recommend their use in personal, family, and group prayer and devotional settings."

Chris Bruno, Global Partner for Hawaii and the Pacific Islands, Training Leaders International; author, *The Whole Story of the Bible in 16 Verses*

"David Murray's new StoryChanger Devotional series is exactly what Christians are craving right now. These daily devotionals are accessible both in their content and brevity. In just a few minutes each day, readers will find comfort in the truth of the gospel and challenges in following the way of Jesus. Just because the devotionals are short doesn't mean that they won't pack a life-changing punch. This series will introduce you to the Bible in the ways that you want and provoke you in the ways that you need."

Adam Griffin, coauthor, *Family Discipleship*; Host, *The Family Discipleship Podcast*; Pastor, Eastside Community Church, Dallas, Texas

"If you struggle to connect the truths of Scripture to your daily life, this book will help you mine Philippians and Colossians for rich theological truth and show you how to put what you've learned into action. David Murray's StoryChanger devotionals are immensely practical and encouraging!"

Glenna Marshall, author, *The Promise Is His Presence* and *Everyday Faithfulness*

T0006713

Philippians and Colossians

The StoryChanger Devotional Series

By David Murray

Exodus: Stories of Redemption and Relationship

Luke: Stories of Mission and Mercy

Philippians and Colossians: Stories of Joy and Identity

Philippians and Colossians

Stories of Joy and Identity

David Murray

WHEATON, ILLINOIS

Library of Congress Cataloging-in-Publication Data

Names: Murray, David, 1966 May 28– author.
Title: Philippians and Colossians : stories of joy and identity / David Murray.
Description: Wheaton, Illinois : Crossway, 2023. | Series: The storychanger devotional | Includes bibliographical references.
Identifiers: LCCN 2022022312 (print) | LCCN 2022022313 (ebook) | ISBN 9781433580970 (trade paperback) | ISBN 9781433580987 (pdf) | ISBN 9781433581007 (epub)
Subjects: LCSH: Bible. Philippians—Commentaries. | Bible. Colossians—Commentaries
Classification: LCC BS2705.53 .M87 2023 (print) | LCC BS2705.53 (ebook) | DDC 227/.607—dc23/eng/20221129
LC record available at https://lccn.loc.gov/2022022312
LC ebook record available at https://lccn.loc.gov/2022022313

Crossway is a publishing ministry of Good News Publishers.

VP		32	31	30	29	28	27	26	25	24	23
15	14	13	12	11	10	9	8	7	6	5	4	3	2	1

Dedicated to Chris "Live from the Betsie" Bosse.
A fishing guide who became my friend and
changed my whole family's story.

Contents

Introduction to the StoryChanger Devotionals

Do you want to know the Bible's Story better, but don't know how? Do you want to change your story, but don't know how? Do you want to share the Bible's Story and the way it has changed your story, but don't know how? The StoryChanger Devotional series is the answer to this triple *how*.

How can I know the Bible better? At different points in my Christian life, I've tried to use various helps to go deeper in personal Bible study, but I found commentaries were too long and technical, whereas study Bibles were too brief and not practical.

How can I change my life for the better? I knew the Bible's Story was meant to change my story but couldn't figure out how to connect God's Story with my story in a transformative way. I was stuck, static, and frustrated at my lack of change, growth, and progress.

How can I share God's Story better? I've often been embarrassed by how slow and ineffective I am at sharing God's Story one-on-one. I know God's Story relates to other people's stories and that God's Story can change others' stories for the better, but I'm reluctant to seek out opportunities and hesitant when they arise.

So how about a series of books that teach us the Bible's Story in a way that helps to change our story and equips us to tell the Story to others? Or, to put it another way, how about books that teach us God's Story in a way that changes ours and others' stories?

After writing *The StoryChanger: How God Rewrites Our Story by Inviting Us into His* as an introduction to Jesus as the transformer of our stories, I thought, "Okay, what now? That's the theory, what about the practice? That's the introduction, but what about the next chapters? Jesus is the StoryChanger, but how can his Story change my story in practical ways on a daily basis? And how do I share his life-changing Story with others?"

I looked for daily devotionals that would take me through books of the Bible in a way that explained God's Story, changed my story, and equipped me to tell God's Story to others in a life-changing way. When I couldn't find any resources that had all three elements, I thought, "I'll write some devotionals for myself to help me know God's Story, change my story, and tell the story to others."

A few weeks later COVID hit, and I decided to start sharing these devotionals with the congregation I was serving at the time. I wanted to keep them connected with God and one another through that painful period of prolonged isolation from church and from one another.

I found that, like myself, people seemed to be hungry for daily devotionals that were more than emotional. They enjoyed daily devotionals that were educational, transformational, and missional. We worked our way verse-by-verse through books of the Bible with a focus on brevity, simplicity, clarity, practicality, and shareability. The StoryChanger started changing our stories with his Story, turning us into storytellers and therefore storychangers too.

Although these devotionals will take only about five minutes a day, I'm not promising you quick fixes. No, the StoryChanger usually changes our stories little by little. But over months and years of exposure to the StoryChanger's Story, he rewrites our story, and, through us, rewrites others' stories too.

To encourage you, I invite you to join the StoryChangers community at www.thestorychanger.life. There you can sign up for the weekly StoryChangers newsletter and subscribe to the StoryChangers podcast. Let's build a community of storychangers, committed Christians who dedicate themselves to knowing God's Story better, being changed by God's Story for the better, and sharing God's Story better. We'll meet the StoryChanger, have our stories changed, and become storychangers. I look forward to meeting you there and together changing stories with God's Story.[1]

---

1 Some of this content originally appeared on the *Living the Bible* podcast, which has since been replaced by *The StoryChanger* podcast, https://podcasts.apple.com/us /podcast/the-storychanger/id1581826891.

Introduction to *Philippians and Colossians: Stories of Joy and Identity*

How can I be happy? is perhaps the most common question in the world. A Google search for the answer produces countless results. But there's only one right answer, and it's found in Paul's letter to the Philippians, often called the epistle of joy.

The answer is certainly not found in our circumstances, as Paul writes about joy from a prison cell. The answer is not found in seeking happiness, as Paul insists it's possible only as a by-product of seeking something (or someone) higher than happiness. The answer is not found in hedonism, as Paul calls the Philippians to ethical purity. Neither is it found in emotionalism, as Paul prioritizes facts over feelings, the mind of Christ over shallow pleasures. Paul's letter to the Philippians tells stories of Christian happiness through Christ-centeredness and Christ-likeness. May the Storychanger's joy-full stories change our sad stories and make us joy-filled storytellers so that we become storychangers too.

Who am I? is another common question in the world. How we view our basic identities, the way we think about ourselves, impacts everything in our lives: our self-image, our health, our spirituality, our ethics, our roles and relationships, our careers, and our view of the past, present, and future. Answer it right, and we flourish. Answer it wrong, and we wither.

The Colossians were answering it wrong because false teachers called Gnostics (literally, "Knowers" or "Know-It-Alls") had infiltrated the infant church and were in the process of stealing the Colossians' God-given identity as complete in Christ. The Gnostic message was "Christ is not enough, therefore you are not enough. You need to add special knowledge through special practices and experiences to be special to God."

Sensing the Colossians' mortal danger of having their God-given identities stolen, Paul reminds the Colossians that Christ is enough, therefore they are enough in Christ; Christ is complete, therefore they are complete in Christ; Christ is special to God, therefore they are special in Christ.

The Colossians were in danger of suffering identity theft, and we're in even greater danger, as multiple identity thieves encircle us: Hollywood, social media, peers, schools, politicians, Satan, and more conspire to tell us various versions of the same story: "Christ is not enough, therefore you are not enough." Let's use God's Story to delete these stories and change our story with God's Story. May these stories of identity change our identity stories and make us storytellers so that we become storychangers too.

PHILIPPIANS

We love others by getting God's love to others.

Hear
God's Story

Change
Your Story

Tell
the Story

Change
Others' Stories

1

Love Language

"How do I tell her I love her?" That question dominated my life about two to three months after I started dating Shona (now my wife of thirty years). Despite glacier-slow beginnings, it didn't take long for me to realize that I did love her and wanted to marry her.

But she didn't know that. I'd been so scared about scaring her off that I hadn't even held her hand yet. And soon she would return to her parents' house in the distant Scottish Highlands for the two-month university break. I racked my brains about the best way to say *I love you*.

The morning she was to leave, I read Philippians 1:3 in my devotions: "I thank my God in all my remembrance of you." "That's it!" I thought. Not too strong, not too vague. I grabbed a ninety-nine-cent card from the store, wrote the verse, and handed it to her as she boarded the bus. I went back home and anxiously wondered whether I'd picked the right verse. Here's what I found in Philippians 1:1–3.

I Want the Best for You 1:1–2

Paul's opening words to the Philippians were, "Grace to you and peace from God our Father and the Lord Jesus Christ" (1:2). If love is wanting the very best for people, then Paul couldn't have expressed his love better. Is there anything greater we could wish for someone than the grace of God? Whenever Paul thought of others, his next thought was, "How can I get God's grace to them?" There is no greater way to love others than to pray God's grace toward them and therefore also God's peace.

We love others by getting God's love to others.

How else did Paul express his love for the Philippians?

I Thank God for You 1:3

Paul loved the Philippians not only by sending *God's* love to them but also by sending *his* love to them. He'd shown them God's heart for them, but Paul also wanted to show his own heart for them. How could he do that when he was in prison many miles away from First Church of Philippi?

He invited them to peek inside his mind and see how he thought about them. "I thank my God in all my remembrance of you" (1:3). He kept them beside him by recalling all his memories of them. As he thought about them, his heart flamed with gratitude to God for them. Paul wasn't afraid or embarrassed to bear his heart in vulnerable expressions of his love for the Philippians (as 1:4–11 also reveals).

When God's grace comes to us, our gratitude goes to him.

Changing Our Story with God's Story

So did my card work? We had no cell phones then, so hours of second-guessing followed. Was it too forward? Or was it too backward? Was she crying on the bus, thinking, "Oh no, this guy loves me"? Or was she crying on the bus, thinking, "I have no idea if this guy loves me." He loves me. He loves me not.

Finally my phone rang. "David, thank you so much for the card. That meant the world to me." I let out a huge sigh of relief. After that phone call, I felt pretty sure I had secured her for that two-month separation. But I resolved that when she came back, I'd pick up the pace, take some risks, somehow hold her hand, and even tell her straight: "I love you!"

Summary: "What's the best way to say 'I love you'?" *Express love by joyfully communicating the grace of God and gratitude to God.*

Question: How will you love like this in your community?

Prayer: God of Grace and Peace, help me to love by giving your grace, so that you will be loved with peaceful and grateful hearts.

Gospel partnership is gospel productivity.

2

Gospel Partnership

PHILIPPIANS 1:4–5

How do I thank God when I have nothing to thank God for? Sometimes we feel like that, don't we? God takes away our loved ones, God takes away our health, God takes away our joy. What's left to thank God for?

The apostle Paul helps us answer this question in Philippians 1:4–6. He was in prison for his faith, and God had taken away his friends and family, his ministry, his comfort, and his freedom. If anyone had reason to be grouchy, it was Paul. Yet he opens his letter with joyful gratitude (1:3–4).

How does he thank God for something when he's got nothing to thank God for? He finds gratitude gas in the tank of gospel partnership (1:5) and gospel perseverance (1:6). We'll consider gospel partnership in this devotional and gospel perseverance in the next.

We Were Partners in the Gospel 1:5

Paul stirs up joyful gratitude by looking back at their "partnership in the gospel from the first day" (1:5). From the first day Paul and the Philippians had met, they had been united in joyful gospel service and labor. Their heads, hearts, and hands had been aligned and allied in the great cause of spreading the gospel. Competition and division were unknown among them as they worked in perfect harmony from day one. All their energies had been devoted and harnessed to evangelism of the lost, a reminder of better days for the now divided Philippians.

They had prayed together, witnessed together, wept together, rejoiced together, fellowshiped together, eaten and drunk together, served together, and worshiped together. The gospel had bonded them in an unforgettable way. Their spiritual partnership had been spiritually productive.

Gospel partnership is gospel productivity.

How long did that partnership last?

We Still Are Partners in the Gospel 1:5

Even though prison bars now separated them, their gospel partnership continued, Paul in prison and the Philippians in Philippi. He wanted them to feel spiritually connected and united to him even though they were spiritually divided and distant from him. Whatever had happened in the intervening years, Paul assured them that their gospel partnership was enduring. They were still united in gospel cooperation, not only on the first day but "until now" (1:5). For that he remains grateful to God and wants to stir up similar gratitude in them.

Gospel partnership superglues gospel friendship.

Changing Our Story with God's Story

Not long after I was converted to Christ in my early twenties, a friend and I started going into homeless men's shelters in Glasgow to share the gospel. I remember, as if it were yesterday, the times of fear-filled prayer we had in the car before going in, and also afterward when we had "survived" and even been blessed in conversations with the men.

Even though I've seen that friend only a few times in the last twenty years, we have a special bond that brings joy every time I think of him. Sharing the gospel together superglued our hearts together in an unforgettable way.

Recently, I met that friend again, and we spent the whole happy time reliving those nights among the homeless men. We felt so much love for one another and gratitude to God through gospel partnership. We were refueled by remembering our gospel partnership.

Summary: How do we thank God when we've got nothing to thank God for? *Revive joyful memories of gospel partnership in the distant past to grow gospel gratitude in the painful present.*

Question: Take some time today to think about or even write about your first mission trip or the first time you partnered with someone in the gospel. How do those experiences affect you now?

Prayer: Heavenly Partner, I am grateful for gospel partnership with you and with my fellow believers. Use gospel partnerships for gospel productivity.

If God starts it, the devil cannot stop it.

 Hear God's Story | Change Your Story | Tell the Story | Change Others' Stories

3

Gospel Perseverance

PHILIPPIANS 1:6

"David, you never stick with anything," my dad said after I decided to give up photography and sell my camera. His comment hit hard and went deep. It was true.

In my early teens, I'd saved up for months to buy an Olympus OM10 SLR camera. Six months after excitedly buying it, I was now selling it in a local newspaper ads section. Prior to that, it was six months of sea fishing. Before that, it was six months of woodworking. Further back, it was six months of making model airplanes. Six months seemed to be when I lost interest and gave up. My dad was right; I never stuck with anything.

Although the comment faded in my late teens (when I got my first job and kept it for five years), it came back with a vengeance when I was converted to Christ in my early twenties. Would this be just another six-month fad? *How could I be sure I would keep going?*

Eventually I shared my fears with a Christian friend and asked him, "How can I be sure I'll keep going?" He took me to Philippians 1:6: "I am sure of this, that he who began a good work in you will bring it to completion at the day of Jesus Christ."

God Started the Work 1:6

The Philippians needed this assurance too. Their beloved Paul was writing to them from prison. The pressure of persecution was mounting, as were problems in the Philippian church. "How can we be sure we'll keep going?" they were probably asking themselves and even each other. Thus, after thanking God for their gospel partnership (1:4–5), Paul thanked God for their gospel perseverance (1:6). In doing so, he reminded them that it was God "who began a good work in you" (1:6).

The Philippians were feeling weak and discouraged. The devil's bad work among them had stalled the church, and it now seemed to be going backward. If they had begun the work, they would have no hope of prevailing. But God started it, and therefore they would continue.

"Don't worry," Paul assured them, "God's good work is greater than the devil's bad work. God has started his good work in your hearts and lives, and that cannot be stopped. If God's started a good work, the devil's bad work can't stop it."

If God starts it, the devil cannot stop it.

How long will God stick at this work?

God Will Finish the Work 1:6

"I am sure of this, that he who began a good work in you will bring it to completion at the day of Jesus Christ" (1:6). Don't you love Paul's certainty here? He's totally confident that what God starts, God will finish. He will never give up, he will never fail. He will hold me tight, he will hold me fast.

How can I be sure I'll keep going? Because God will keep going. If I had begun this work, I wouldn't stick with it. But God began this work, so he'll stick with it. I may feel like giving up, but he never feels like giving up, and he never will.

God's never stopped anything he's started.

Changing Our Story with God's Story

The devil stalled my own faith with this fear of failing, of giving up. I didn't want to tell anyone I was a Christian because I was afraid I couldn't keep it up. But Paul's confidence in this verse gave me confidence to trust God that he would keep me up.

Whether you are just starting on the Christian life or far advanced, I hope my story and the Philippians' story changes your story from fear of faltering to confidence in completion.

Summary: How can I be sure I'll keep going with God? I can be sure that God will keep going with me. *Build your stickability on God's stickability to remove fear and fuel joy.*

Question: Who can you encourage with this truth?

Prayer: Preserver, thank you for starting your good work in me. I trust that what you've started, you will finish.

By grace God says to us, "I love you." So by grace we can say to each other, "I love you."

Hear
God's Story | Change
Your Story | Tell
the Story | Change
Others' Stories

4

I Love You

PHILIPPIANS 1:7–8

I've lost count of the number of people who have told me that their parents never told them that they loved them. They usually say something like, "I don't think my dad or mom ever told me that they loved me. I mean, they showed it, but they never said it."

I grew up in a culture where love was clearly shown but rarely spoken. It was my wife, Shona, who taught me how to say "I love you," both to each other and to our children. I don't think we ever talk on the phone or say goodbye to our kids now without saying "I love you." And they say it back. I love hearing those words, and I've learned to love saying them too.

How do we learn to say "I love you"? Shona's example helped me. But we also have Paul's example in Philippians 1:7–8.

I Hold You in My Heart 1:7

"It is right for me to feel this way about you all, because I hold you in my heart" (1:7). When I hear Paul say, "I hold you in my heart," I picture his heart with two hands reaching out, grasping the Philippians and holding them as tightly, warmly, and affectionately as possible. Prison meant he couldn't hold them in his physical hands, but he assured them he held them with his heart hands—and wasn't letting go.

This wasn't just natural love; it was also spiritual love. Paul sourced it in gospel grace, gospel mission, and gospel suffering. "For you are all partakers with me of grace, both in my imprisonment and in the defense and confirmation of the gospel" (1:7).

They got God's grace together, they were on mission for God's grace together, and they suffered for God's grace together. Paul loved them by grace, because of grace, and for the sake of grace. The Romans could imprison Paul, but they couldn't imprison his love.

By grace God says to us, "I love you."
So by grace we can say to each other, "I love you."

Where did Paul get this unstoppable love?

I Yearn for You with the Affection of Jesus 1:8

What a stunning expression: "I yearn for you all with the affection of Christ Jesus" (1:8). Think about how Jesus yearns for his people and feels for his people. "For God is my witness," says Paul. What a dazzling declaration of devotion! What a lovely lesson in love!

The yearning we feel for our fellow Christians is a pale imitation of the yearning Jesus has for us. It's great to feel a yearning for Christians and the yearning of Christians. It's even better to feel a yearning for Jesus and, best of all, to feel Jesus's yearning for us. Even if we're not that emotional, we can learn to yearn. The more we feel Jesus's yearning for us, the more we will yearn for Jesus's people too.

We can yearn for others because Jesus yearns for us.

Changing Our Story with God's Story

I remember hearing of a Christian woman who grew frustrated that her husband never said "I love you." At the most, he would reply, "Me too," or, "You too" (whatever that means). Exasperated, one day she exploded, "Why do you never tell me that you love me?" He replied, "Listen, just assume that I love you, and if it ever changes I'll let you know." How unlike Paul or Jesus! How much happier we would all be if we could learn to say "I love you."

Summary: How do we learn to say "I love you"? *Open your lips with grace-filled "I love yous" by opening your heart to God's grace-filled "I love yous."*

Question: Whom do you know that needs to be cheered by hearing your grace-filled and Christlike "I love you"?

Prayer: Loving Lord, thank you for loving me and yearning for me. Help me to share that joy by loving and yearning for you and your people.

As long as we
live more, we
can love more.

 Hear
God's Story | Change
Your Story | Tell
the Story | Change
Others' Stories

5

The Secret to Productivity

PHILIPPIANS 1:9–11

"How can I be more productive?" Most of us have asked that question, haven't we? Or maybe we have employees, students, or kids, and our question is, "How can I make *them* more productive?" We ask these questions because more productivity usually means more success and more money, or less time at work and more leisure. Ideally both, right?

So we read books, listen to podcasts, and attend seminars about how to be more productive. We learn better time management, better energy management, better task management, better project management, better schedule management, better employee management, and so on. More prioritizing, more reorganizing, more incentivizing, and on and on it goes. And, somehow, we still seem to end up with more work but less money and less time.

How can I be more productive? The secret is more love. Let's look at how Paul connects love and spiritual productivity in Philippians 1:9–11.

Abounding Love Is the Cause 1:9

Paul's first prayer for the Philippians was "that your love may abound more and more" (1:9). His first prayer for them wasn't more money, more success, more friends, more comfort, or more health, but more love. Love for whom? Love for Christ and love for his people.

How much more? *More and more.* May your love overflow like a flooded river, increase like inflation, multiply like crypto, escalate like an elevator, grow like bamboo. There's no limit to love. It never tops out, reaches a ceiling, or plateaus. However much we've loved, there's more to love.

As long as we live more, we can love more.

What's the result of this love?

Abounding Productivity Is the Effect 1:9–11

Why does Paul want their love to swell and spread? It wasn't just so they could feel warm and fuzzy emotions (although there's nothing wrong with warm and fuzzy emotions). It was so that they would be more spiritually productive.

More love means more spiritual knowledge and discernment: "That your love may abound more and more, with knowledge and all discernment" (1:9). If they loved more, they would know more and make better decisions.

More love means more spiritual excellence, purity, and confidence: "So that you may approve what is excellent, and so be pure and blameless for the day of Christ" (1:10). An increase in love would increase their standards, holiness, and assurance.

More love means more spiritual fruit: "Filled with the fruit of righteousness that comes through Jesus Christ" (1:11). Loving soil grows large trees with fruit-laden branches.

More love means more glory and praise of God: "To the glory and praise of God" (1:11). As love is magnified, so is God and his worship.

I once asked an author who seemed like a writing machine, "How do you produce so much?" "I love what I do, David." That's it, isn't it? When we love something, it doesn't even feel like work. Love makes everything easier.

The Philippians needed to hear this message because their divisions were diminishing their productivity. Love oils the machine of productivity, but arguments are like grit in the gears.

When love surges, productivity soars.

Changing Our Story with God's Story

Jesus was the most productive person who ever lived because he was the most loving person who ever lived. His abounding love resulted in abounding productivity. His perfect love meant perfect productivity, perfect knowledge and discernment, perfect excellence, purity, and confidence, perfect fruits of righteousness, and perfect glory and praise to God.

When my love is low and my spiritual productivity is poor, I put my trust in his lovely love and perfect productivity. That not only deletes my past but it also lights my love and restarts my fruit factory.

Summary: How can I be more productive? *Pray for more passion for more productivity.*

Question: How will you increase your love for God, his people, your neighbors, and your enemies?

Prayer: Lord, make my love abound more and more so that my productivity will soar and soar on the wings of joy.

Failure opens its pockets when we are open about failure.

6

Picking the Pocket of Failure

PHILIPPIANS 1:12–14

"Invite failure in, embrace it, then pick its pocket." So says the Dilbert cartoonist Scott Adams in his bestselling biography, *How to Fail at Almost Everything and Still Win Big* (Portfolio, 2013). His point is that failure comes with big pockets full of value if we would welcome it, embrace it, and learn lessons from it.

That's what the apostle Paul did two thousand years ago when his gospel mission "failed" and he ended up jailed. Let's see what Paul finds in failure's pockets in Philippians 1:12–14, as he encourages us with his answer to the question, *How should I deal with personal setbacks?*

The Gospel Takes One Step Backward 1:12

You go into work one day only to be told that the business owner, your boss, was arrested and jailed last night. What now? Crowds of concerned employees gather around watercoolers to discuss how to keep the company running, or at least stop it from collapsing. Others are uploading their resumes online.

Clients, suppliers, and customers jam the phone lines as the word spreads throughout the business community. Your closest competitors are already moving in for the kill. You're afraid, you're annoyed at your boss, you're doubting yourself, and you're questioning God's providence.

Welcome to First Church of Philippi as they receive word that their founding pastor is holed up in a Roman jail. The apostle Paul doesn't try to hide or sugarcoat the reality: "I want you to know, brothers, that what has happened to me . . ." (1:12). Yes, the rumors are true: I'm in jail. Paul owns it, admits it, accepts it. This is bad. He starts with the terrible truth.

Failure opens its pockets when we are open about failure.

How does Paul reframe this to help the Philippians recover their balance?

The Gospel Takes Two Steps Forward 1:12–14

Yes, this is a setback, but God has used it to move the gospel forward. It "has really served to advance the gospel" (1:12). How so?

The first step forward, Paul explains, is that "it has become known throughout the whole imperial guard and to all the rest that my imprisonment is for Christ" (1:13). Throughout the garrison, groups of solders were gathered around waterpots, discussing this weird prisoner who wouldn't stop talking about Jesus. Every time they brought him bread and water, he talked about Jesus. When they passed his cell, he was talking to Jesus. They checked his cell regularly to make sure he really was in there alone. They'd never had such a happy, contented prisoner. Who was this Jesus he was obsessed with?

The second step forward was that "most of the brothers, having become confident in the Lord by my imprisonment, are much more bold to speak the word without fear" (1:14). Instead of sowing doubt, Paul's confidence emboldened his fellow gospel laborers to speak about Jesus free of fear. Paul's reaction to this setback propelled them forward. As Paul's ministry took one step back, they took multiple steps forward. A setback need not be a step back. A setback can be a step forward.

Jailing the gospel frees the gospel.

Changing Our Story with God's Story

Take off the gold self-centered frames labeled *personal loss*, *personal pain*, and *personal plans*, and put on the wooden cross-centered frame of gospel opportunity. The picture is the same, but it looks way better when framed with blood-stained wood. When we're forced to take a step back, let's look for gospel opportunities and gospel advances. Invite failure in, embrace it, and pick its pockets. Then what made you sad will make you glad.

Summary: How should I deal with personal setbacks? *Reframe personal setbacks as opportunities for gospel advances.*

Question: What setback can you reframe with the gospel so that you go forward rather than backward?

Prayer: Heavenly Eye Doctor, give me new gospel frames so that I am not overcome but rather an overcomer.

We preach the love
of Christ, out of love
for Christ, to increase
love for Christ.

Hear
God's Story

Change
Your Story

Tell
the Story

Change
Others' Stories

7

Fallen (or Falling) Preachers

PHILIPPIANS 1:15–18

"My favorite preacher has fallen. What now?" Perhaps this has happened to you. It seems like almost every few months another well-known preacher bites the dust.

It's perplexing and confusing, isn't it? These men preached sound sermons and wrote good books. Do I now discount and deny all the benefit I got from them over the years? Do I stop listening to their sermons and reading their books? Can I separate the words from the person who spoke or wrote them? *How do we relate to fallen preachers?* Let's see how Paul faced that dilemma in Philippians 1:15–18.

Most Preach Christ to Benefit Others 1:15–16

Paul was silenced in prison, but he was encouraged that others in Philippi were still speaking of Christ. Out of love for Christ, for Paul, and for the Philippians, men stepped up to preach Christ "from good will . . . out of love, knowing that I am put here for the defense of the gospel" (1:15–16). They preached the best of messages with the best of motives. Denying themselves, they wanted the best for Christ, for Paul, and for the Philippians.

*We preach the love of Christ, out of love for Christ,
to increase love for Christ.*

Are some preachers out for themselves and not others?

Some Preach Christ to Benefit Themselves 1:15–18

Paul had no time for those who preached a false Christ. His letters are full of fighting against false teaching. But how did he respond to those who preached the right Christ for the wrong reasons and with wrong motives? Some of them were operating in First Church of Philippi. "Some indeed preach Christ from envy and rivalry . . . out of selfish ambition, not sincerely but thinking to afflict me in my imprisonment" (1:15–17).

They preached the right message but with the wrong motives. They were driven by jealousy and ambition. They preached to promote themselves and demote Paul. They said all the right words but had all the wrong reasons for them. They preached the selfless Christ selfishly, the humble Christ proudly.

So did Paul pray for the selfless preachers and condemn the selfish? That's probably what we would do. If we had our cellphones in our cells, we would be attacking these self-centered scammers on Twitter, Facebook, and YouTube. But if Paul were alive today, he would be pressing "like," "heart," and "retweet" every time they posted something true about Christ. Look at verse 18: "What then? Only that in every way, whether in pretense or in truth, Christ is proclaimed, and in that I rejoice. Yes, and I will rejoice" (1:18).

It's stunning, isn't it? Selfless words were on their lips, while selfish motives were in their hearts. But every time Christ was proclaimed, whatever the motive of the preacher, Paul was jumping for joy in jail.

Rejoice if Christ is made known,
even if the preacher's making himself known.

Changing Our Story with God's Story

Maybe it's not that our favorite preacher has fallen, but that our own pastor is falling in our estimation. We're beginning to see things that concern us: his lifestyle, his vanity, his self-promotion, or his love of controversy. We're uneasy and concerned, but he still seems to preach Christ and faithfully explain God's word. What do we do with that? Like Paul, we jump with joy that Christ is preached and leave the motivations for God to sort out.

Summary: How do we relate to fallen (or falling) preachers? *Jump for joy every time Christ is preached, regardless of the preacher's motive.*

Question: How can you learn to jump higher when Christ is preached?

Prayer: Faithful God, keep me faithful so that I do not fall either in message or motivation, and show me how to serve Christ for his glory and others' good, rather than my own.

Living is Christ.
Dying is more Christ.

 Hear God's Story | Change Your Story | Tell the Story | Change Others' Stories

8

Delivered from Death or through Death?

PHILIPPIANS 1:19–21

Have you ever viewed death as a deliverance rather than a defeat? Paul did. He was in jail, and his beloved First Church of Philippi was in trouble. Rival pastors were fighting each other (1:15–18), the believers were fighting each other (1:27), and external opponents were fighting them all (1:28–29). *How will God get me out of this?* the Philippians asked each other.

In Philippians 1:19–21, Paul answers with a surprising view of deliverance that can help us when we can't see a way out.

God May Deliver Us in This Life 1:19–20

Paul was praying for his deliverance. The Philippians were praying for his deliverance. The Spirit of Jesus Christ was praying for his deliverance. "I know that through your prayers and the help of the Spirit of Jesus Christ this will turn out for my deliverance" (1:19).

Confident that he would be delivered, Paul therefore shunned shame to honor Christ in his body all his days. "It is my eager expectation and hope that I will not be at all ashamed, but that with full courage now as always Christ will be honored in my body, whether by life . . ." (1:20).

Daily life is a daily deliverance.

Eventually, after he serves Christ faithfully
and courageously in jail,
God will answer Paul's prayer,
and he'll get his life back then. Right?

God Will Deliver Us by Death 1:20–21

Paul recognized that all these prayers for deliverance could have a surprising answer. Instead of delivered to life, he might be delivered by death. That's right; Paul sees death as a deliverance not a defeat, an answer to prayer not a failed prayer. "That with full courage now as always Christ will be honored in my body, whether by life or by death. For to me to live is Christ, and to die is gain" (1:20–21).

He asks for courage to lift up Christ by his life or by his death. He sees that deliverance may mean living for Christ as a prisoner in jail, living with Christ as a free man in Philippi, or living as a holy saint with Christ in heaven. And for Paul, there's no question which is the greatest deliverance. It's the deliverance of death, because death delivers more of Christ than life does. "For to me to live is Christ, and to die is gain" (1:21).

Living is Christ.
Dying is more Christ.

Changing Our Story with God's Story

I've been in a few desperate situations in my life. One of the worst was when I was diagnosed with multiple blood clots in my lungs and the doctor warned me, "Don't move; you have a life-threatening illness." In the coming hours I prayed for life as I'd never prayed before.

But there were also moments when God gave me a great peace, and even a joy, about leaving this world and entering the next, if that was his will (though my wife wasn't very happy when I told her this!). When I thought of Jesus suffering for my sins on the cross, I especially felt delivered from fear and deluged with joyful confidence.

Maybe you're facing cancer or depression or bankruptcy or persecution, and you're asking, "How will God get me out of this?" Let's shun shame, call for courage, and honor Christ, whether he gives us a mini-deliverance in this life or a mega-deliverance through death, and find joy in both.

Summary: How will God get me out of this? *Pray for deliverance with confidence that God will deliver you for Christ in this life or to Christ in death.*

Question: Whom do you know that needs this message of deliverance, and how will you get it to them?

Prayer: Deliverer, deliver me in life or deliver me by death in a way that maximizes honor for Christ.

Living for Christ is good; living with Christ is better.

9

A Useful Life or Eternal Life?

PHILIPPIANS 1:22-26

James longs for heaven and often expresses the wish to die young so that he can get there early. Susan loves life and doesn't like thinking about heaven too much because there's so much kingdom work to be done on earth.

Most of us are varying mixtures of James and Susan, creating at times a confusing and painful tension. Sometimes we feel guilty about how little we long for heaven; other times we feel guilty that our desire for heaven is merely escapism from this world's troubles. *How do we balance our longing for eternal life with our longing for a useful life?*

In Philippians 1:22–26 Paul, a James/Susan mix, models the answer for us.

We Want to Depart for Heaven 1:22-23

Although Paul always held a degree of painful tension, he was clear about what he wanted most for himself. "If I am to live in the flesh, that means fruitful labor for me. Yet which I shall choose I cannot tell. I am hard pressed between the two. My desire is to depart and be with Christ, for that is far better" (1:22–23).

Paul's greatest wish was to depart earth and arrive in heaven. This wasn't mere escapism from the troubles of this world. He wasn't thinking so much about what he would leave behind but what he was going to. He was going to be with Christ, which would be far better than anything this life could offer. Jesus was Paul's greatest passion and pleasure. He knew he would get more of Jesus in heaven; therefore, he wanted heaven more than earth.

Living for Christ is good;
living with Christ is better.

What if God doesn't give us
heaven anytime soon?

We Are Willing to Stay on Earth 1:24–26

Given the choice, Paul would go to heaven. But Paul was not a man ruled by his passions and preferences. Rather, he was a man who asked God continually, "What will you have me to do?" He knew what he wanted, but he wanted what God wanted even more.

When he asked that question of God, he got his answer: "If I am to live in the flesh, that means fruitful labor for me. . . . To remain in the flesh is more necessary on your account. Convinced of this, I know that I will remain and continue with you all, for your progress and joy in the faith, so that in me you may have ample cause to glory in Christ Jesus, because of my coming to you again" (1:22, 24–26).

God wanted Paul to continue living and serving, because the Philippians needed him if they were to continue progressing in faith and rejoicing in faith. Also, if God spared him to return to First Church of Philippi, that would produce an extraordinary outpouring of glory to God. There was much fruitful labor left for Paul in this life.

We want heaven for our benefit,
but we're willing to wait, for others' benefit.

Changing Our Story with God's Story

Most of us need to multiply our James but also add to our Susan. If you need more of James's heavenliness in your life, take one minute a day to think of heaven. Set a timer for sixty seconds and think about what heaven will be like. One minute of daily life thinking about eternal life will change our view of both our daily life and our eternal life. If you need more of Susan's earthiness, ask Jesus every day, "Lord, what will you have me to do?"

Summary: How do we balance our longing for eternal life with our longing for a useful life? *Cultivate the greatest longing for eternal life with Christ, but balance it with a willingness to live a useful life for Christ.*

Question: Do you need more of James or Susan in your life? What are you doing to get the right James/Susan balance?

Prayer: Lord of Heaven and Earth, help me to long joyfully for heaven but live joyfully for you on earth while I wait.

Diseases can kill the body, but division can kill the soul.

Hear
God's Story

Change
Your Story

Tell
the Story

Change
Others' Stories

10

Fight for Peace

PHILIPPIANS 1:27

Throughout history, churches have faced many hardships that have threatened the unity of their people. The challenges of COVID-19 is a recent example. This global pandemic was a difficult time for many churches.

Churches had to figure out how to apply biblical commands to "honor one another" while navigating the complexities of life during a pandemic. It was an opportunity for the devil to undermine hard-won chuch unity.

But is the fight for church unity worth the effort? If it is, then how should we fight for church unity? Paul guides us in Philippians 1:27.

Fight to Unite Your Hearts 1:27

What does a life worthy of the gospel of Christ look like? It looks like a life that fights for united love. "Only let your manner of life be worthy of the gospel of Christ, so that whether I come and see you or am absent, I may hear of you that you are standing firm in one spirit" (1:27). "Standing firm in one spirit" is the resolute determination to maintain love and affection for one another. No matter how much Satan tries to divide us, we're going to beat him, not be beaten by him.

Paul doesn't view unity as something for softies or wimps, but as a mark of strength and valor. It usually takes more courage to unite than it does to divide. Dividing is easy; uniting is hard. Division happens without effort, but unity takes maximum effort.

Division isn't something we can live with.
Division will take our lives.

How do we unite our hearts?

Fight to Unite Your Minds 1:27

We win the battle to keep our hearts together by fighting the battle to keep our minds together: "With one mind striving side by side for the faith of the gospel" (1:27).

If our minds are focused most on controversy, that's a recipe for disastrous disunity. But if we can keep our minds most on the faith of the gospel, then our minds will be "side by side" rather than far apart or fighting one another.

Again, notice the aggressive language Paul uses: "With one mind *striving* side by side for the faith of the gospel" (1:27). Striving involves work, sweat, pain, tears, determination, and discipline. That's how much effort is required to stay united. It takes striving to keep our minds most on the faith of the gospel. That's radical and rigorous spirituality. That's the kind of activism we need.

Diseases can kill the body, but division can kill the soul.

Changing Our Story with God's Story

Many of us reserve our fighting spirit for attacking other Christians who differ from us. That's certainly a fast track to macho status in some circles. But Paul says it often takes more courage to fight for unity than to fight fellow believers.

Unity was of utmost importance to Jesus. He calls us to "become perfectly one" (John 17:23). Therefore, let's fight to unite.

Summary: How should we fight for church unity? *Fight with all your might for gospel unity to enjoy church unity.*

Question: What can you do to advance unity of mind and heart among Christians today?

Prayer: Lord, you are our head and we are your body. Help us to fight the viruses that infect your body rather than fight the members of your body.

Suffering for Christ is a gift from Christ.

11

The Surprising Gift of Suffering

PHILIPPIANS 1:28–30

Friends of mine in the UK have parents who have been missionaries in Afghanistan for the last ten years. During the American military withdrawal from that country in 2021, the parents found themselves hiding for their lives. The family wrote of their parents: "They have led countless people to Jesus. Most of whom will meet him in the coming days."

"Just FaceTimed with my parents," wrote one of the family members on social media. "They are hiding, surrounded by gunfire and bombs. Everyone is hiding in their homes. The Taliban are taking women and slaughtering anyone who resists them. They will kill all foreigners and anyone who has worked with foreigners over the past 20 years. Yet my mum and dad are full of peace and joy."

What? Full of peace and joy, while surrounded by bombs and bullets? Full of peace and joy, knowing that they are about to be killed?

How were they suffering for Christ without fear? *How can we suffer for Christ without fear?* Philippians 1:28–30 explains how. It starts with "not frightened in anything by your opponents" (1:28). How is that possible? Paul reframes suffering to remove fear.

Suffering for Christ Is a Proof 1:28

"This [persecution of Christians] is a clear sign to them of their destruction, but of your salvation, and that from God" (1:28).

Paul assured the Philippians that their enemies were persecuting them for their faith, and that they were suffering for their faith. This proved that their persecutors were doomed to destruction by God, but the Philippians were destined for salvation by God.

**Persecution for our faith is
an assurance of our faith.**

*Is suffering for Christ a
punishment from Christ?*

Suffering for Christ Is a Gift 1:29

"For it has been granted [or gifted] to you that for the sake of Christ you should not only believe in him but also suffer for his sake" (1:29). A gift? How is suffering for Christ a gift? It feels more like a punishment than a present. That may be how it feels, but God's word tells us how to think differently in order to feel differently. It says that we should be as grateful for the privilege of suffering for Christ as we are for the gift of believing in Christ. God's sovereign grace is equally at work in both the gift of believing in Christ and the gift of suffering for Christ. That's how the apostles reframed suffering too, rejoicing that they were counted worthy to suffer dishonor for Christ's name (see Acts 5:41).

**Suffering for Christ is
a gift from Christ.**

*An example of this would help a lot.
Do we have one?*

Suffering for Christ Is a Model 1:30

"Engaged in the same conflict that you saw I had and now hear that I still have" (1:30). Paul was an inspiring example of fearless suffering for the faith. And the Philippians could be inspiring examples to others too. Willingness to suffer for Christ encourages others to suffer for Christ.

We are supermodels of super-suffering.

Changing Our Story with God's Story

I often ask people, "What's your aim in your Christian life?" Or, "What would you like to do or be in the next five to ten years of your Christian life?" I've never had anyone say, "I want to suffer for Christ more." However, if we could see suffering as Paul saw it—a proof of salvation, a gift from Christ, and a model for others—we would have more believers asking for it. In suffering, we gain more than we lose.

Summary: How can we suffer for Christ without fear? *Reframe suffering for Christ as a proof, as a gift, and as a model to replace fear with peace and joy.*

Question: What will you do, additionally or differently, as a result of this message?

Prayer: Suffering Savior, thank you for suffering for me. Help me to suffer for you with peace and joy.

Winning opponents is better than beating them.

12

Church Unity via Christian Humility

PHILIPPIANS 2:1-4

I experienced a terrible church split when I lived and ministered in Scotland. My Presbyterian denomination, which had existed for centuries, was gradually torn apart over a period of ten years until it ruptured completely in January 2000 over theological and moral issues.

It was a troubling time with disastrous consequences that devastated individual lives, marriages, families, and churches for years to come. A few years after the split a counselor told me that his office had been overwhelmed with depressed and anxious Christians from both sides of the divide.

Sometimes church division is inevitable, but unity is preferable if possible. *How can we promote church unity?* The apostle Paul's one-word answer is *humility*. Unity is sourced in humility and humility serves unity. But he used more than one word to persuade First Church of Philippi toward this unity in Philippians 2:1-4.

Christian Unity Is a Miracle 2:1-2

Every united Christian church is a miracle of grace. When we think about how much the devil tries to divide and destroy churches, and how much divisiveness exists in the human heart, it's stunning that any church lasts one Sunday.

That's why Paul asks the Philippians to "complete my joy by being of the same mind, having the same love, being in full accord, and of one mind" (2:2). He wants them to have one mind, one love, one faith, one direction, and one aim, so that he can have full joy. One of Paul's greatest sources of happiness was unity among Christians. This topped off his joy. It was the cream on the milk for him.

He also points them to the resources needed to secure unity: encouragement in Christ, comfort from love, participation in the Spirit, and their affection for and sympathy with one another (2:1). All of these are miraculous results of God's supernatural grace and therefore must be prayed for.

Christian unity is a joy-full miracle.

What's the secret to Christian unity?

Christian Unity Is from Humility 2:3-4

"Do nothing from selfish ambition or conceit," Paul says (2:3). Why? Because every act done or word spoken from self-promotion or self-love is a unity shredder. It's not enough to do the right things; they must also be done in the right way.

Instead of doing the right things in a wrong way, Paul urges, "In humility count others more significant than yourselves. Let each of you look not only to his own interests, but also to the interests of others" (2:3-4).

This is so hard to actually practice, isn't it? In fact, there's nothing harder. We put down and look down on our opponents. But Paul encouraged a default of looking up to them and seeking their good ahead of our own. That doesn't mean becoming a doormat for false teachers or treating wolves like sheep. It means that we enter arguments with fellow Christians preferring to be proven wrong rather than proven right. It means disagreeing without disunity. It's trying to win our opponents' hearts rather than beating our opponents' heads.

Winning opponents is better than beating them.

Changing Our Story with God's Story

God is the great uniter. If he can unite us with himself through Christ, he can unite us with one another through Christ. If he can bridge the biggest chasm of our sins, he can bridge smaller gaps between his people. Jesus laid down his life to be the bridge for sinners to a holy God. Therefore, we can lay down our lives to be the bridge between sinning saints.

Summary: How can I promote Christian unity? *Promote the joy of Christian unity by pursuing the joy of Christian humility.*

Question: Think of a Christian you look down on. How can you look up to him instead?

Prayer: Uniter, make me a joyful bridge by doing a miraculous work of humility in my mind and heart.

Jesus gave up his rights as God to make us right with God.

13

Our Right to Give Up Our Rights

PHILIPPIANS 2:5-8

Think about the humblest person you've ever known. Don't you want to be like that? While the world boasts about pride, the Christian glories in humility. Humility is beautiful. Pride is ugly. The most beautiful Christians I've ever met have been full of humility and empty of self. *But how do I get humility?* Thankfully Paul shows us in Philippians 2:5-8.

Paul has called First Church of Philippi to unity through humility. Their next question, though, is, "How?" Paul points the Philippians to Christ's mind. "Have this mind among yourselves, which is yours in Christ Jesus" (2:5). Think like Jesus did. A Jesus outlook will produce a Jesus outcome; a Jesus attitude will result in Jesus actions. A Jesus mind will be seen in Jesus manners. So what did Jesus think about all the time? He tells us in these verses.

Jesus Gave Up His Rights for Us 2:6

We hear a lot of talk today about human rights, equal rights, my rights, and so on. While some of this is commendable, such talk almost always ends up in conflict and division, because one person's rights will compete with another's. These kinds of "rights fights" were causing division in First Church of Philippi.

Jesus had a different approach to life altogether. "Though he was in the form of God, [he] did not count equality with God a thing to be grasped" (2:6). He was God and had all the rights of God, but he didn't insist on his rights. He didn't view them as something to cling on to at all costs and in all circumstances. He didn't surrender his deity but surrendered his right to be treated like deity.

Jesus gave up his rights as God
to make us right with God.

What kind of rights did he give up?

Jesus Gave Up His Reputation for Us 2:7

"But [he] emptied himself, by taking the form of a servant, being born in the likeness of men" (2:7). He had the highest reputation possible (God) but gave it up and took the lowest reputation possible (slave).

How did he do this? He did not give up being God but gave up his being known as God. He did this not by subtracting his Godhead but by adding humanity—humbled and lowly humanity.

Jesus didn't fight for top billing
but for bottom billing.

How low did Jesus go?

Jesus Gave Up His Royalty for Us 2:8

If reincarnation were true, who would you like to come back as? A president? A billionaire? A king or queen? That's what most people answer when asked that rather silly question.

Jesus was a King, but in his incarnation he took the lowest status. "And being found in human form, he humbled himself by becoming obedient to the point of death, even death on a cross" (2:8). He humbled himself by taking our nature, then humbled himself even further in that nature. The commander became the commanded. The lawgiver became the law-obeyer.

Sometimes we are humbled, usually against our will. It was Jesus's will to be humbled throughout his life and especially in his death. He could have died a heroic death but chose to die a cursed and shameful death.

The lowest death ever reveals
the lowliest mind ever.

Changing Our Story with God's Story

Can you imagine how this mindset would change First Church of Philippi? Now imagine the transformation in your own church. Now do more than imagine it. Image it. Image it by imagining it. The mind of Jesus will make you a model of Jesus.

Summary: How do I get humility? *Think about how to give up your rights, your reputation, and your rule, as Jesus did willingly and joyfully.*

Question: How will you joyfully give up your rights for the good of others?

Prayer: Most High, you became the most low. Give me your lowly heart and mind so that I can live a lowly life.

Talk about Christ more to talk about Christians less.

Hear
God's Story | Change
Your Story | Tell
the Story | Change
Others' Stories

14

Knees and Tongues, Prayer and Praise

PHILIPPIANS 2:9-11

We're living in days of disunity, including Christian disunity. I'm not referring to the historic interchurch disunity that flows from denominational divisions and splits. We now have inner-church disunity being caused by politics and a variety of social concerns.

We will probably never fully agree on our world's deeply complex, personal, and politicized matters. Do we therefore give up and accept the disunity? *How can Christians unite while disagreeing about important issues?* Is that possible? Yes. Finding something far more important to agree on will vaporize our squabbles. That's what Paul does in Philippians 2:9-11.

Every Knee Will Bend 2:9-10

In Philippians 2:5-8, Paul promotes unity by appealing to Jesus's *first* coming. Unite, Paul says, because Jesus gave up his rights, his reputation, and his royalty for the good of his people.

In 2:9-11, Paul promotes unity by appealing to Christ's *second* coming. Unite here and now, Paul says, because we will be united there and then.

Jesus gave up his riches for rags, so God gave him riches for his rags. "Therefore God has highly exalted him and bestowed on him the name that is above every name" (2:9). That highest name is not yet fully acknowledged in the world, but it will be: "So that at the name of Jesus every knee should bow, in heaven and on earth and under the earth" (2:10).

Christians will be fully and totally united at the second coming. Everyone's knee will be equally and unitedly bent in bowing to Christ's lordship. Paul reminds the Philippians of this future united knee-bending to encourage present united knee-bending.

Bent knees straighten
bent relationships.

But do you know what
he said/she said/they said about me?

Every Tongue Will Confess 2:11

Although Christian tongues in Philippi were dividing the church through false doctrine and false accusation, the day is coming when every tongue will say exactly the same thing. "Every tongue [will] confess that Jesus Christ is Lord, to the glory of God the Father" (2:11).

Philippian tongues were speaking about anything but Jesus, dishonoring God in the process. But on the last day, every Christian tongue will cry in unison "Jesus Christ is Lord" to the glory of God the Father. So we might as well practice now. Paul reminds the Philippians of this future united tongue-confessing to encourage present united tongue-confessing. If we talk about one another more than Christ, we've lost sight of Christ.

Talk about Christ more
to talk about Christians less.

Changing Our Story with God's Story

When we're tempted to divide from Christians because of disagreement on relatively trivial matters, we must recall the most important matter—we will kneel beside one another one day and together confess that Jesus Christ is Lord to the glory of God the Father. When we pray and praise together, we unite together.

I've been slandered by other Christians and been sorely tempted to retaliate in kind. However, this passage reminds me that one day our tongues will unite to praise our Savior rather than tear each other apart. As long as I can keep my focus on that future glorified tongue of my brother, I can keep control of my own. Better to confess Christ with my tongue than have sins to confess to Christ about my tongue.

Summary: How can Christians unite while disagreeing about various issues? *Joyfully unite here and now because we will be joyfully united there and then.*

Question: How will you use prayer and praise to unite with other Christians?

Prayer: Praiseworthy Savior, unite me with yourself and other Christians by uniting us in prayer and praise.

God's work *in* guarantees we work *out*.

 Hear God's Story | Change Your Story | Tell the Story | Change Others' Stories

15

A Workout That Works Out

PHILIPPIANS 2:12–13

"My workout isn't working out." A few months ago, one of my friends started working out again. He was really committed, working out at the gym five days a week. Lots of effort, pain, sweat, blood, and tears.

Two months in, his weight had hardly dropped, his muscles had hardly grown, and he was discouraged. "All that work, and nothing to show for it," he moaned. I tried to encourage him that if he kept working at it, he would eventually see some change. But, I have to be honest, I wasn't sure. Some people just can't seem to lose weight. Others can't seem to put on muscle (I'm one of them).

Sometimes we feel the same about holiness. We're working hard at putting off bad habits and putting on new habits, but we still don't seem to make any progress. All that work, and nothing to show for it. *How do we keep working on holiness, when holiness isn't working?* When it comes to holiness, we can be sure our work will pay off, because God's word is sure in Philippians 2:12–13.

We Work Out 2:12

"Therefore, my beloved, as you have always obeyed, so now, not only as in my presence but much more in my absence, work out your own salvation with fear and trembling" (2:12).

"Work out your own salvation." Notice Paul doesn't say "work *for* your salvation." God has done that saving work already. Also "work out your own salvation" does not mean "figure out your own salvation." God has done that too for us.

"Work out your own salvation" means "you've been saved without works. Now work on moral and spiritual progress." We are passive in getting salvation from sin but not in growing in salvation from sin. *Work* speaks of hard, continuous effort and activity. "Pursue, fight, strive, press on to greater and greater obedience regardless of whether or not I am there with you," Paul is saying.

This action of work is to be done with an attitude of awe. Work out your own salvation *with fear and trembling*. Reverence for God will make us eager to do what is right and pleasing to him.

This workout will work out.

How can I be sure my workout
will work out?

Because God Works In 2:13

"For it is God who works in you, both to will and to work for his good pleasure" (2:13). God doesn't work just at the beginning of salvation then leave the rest to us. It is God who keeps working and, because he works, we work. He works in us so that we *want* to obey him and *work* to obey him.

God doesn't force us to go against our wills, but his force changes our wills. His work *in* gives us the will and the ability to work *out*. God gets good pleasure from working on our wills so that we will want to work to please him.

Imprisoned Paul cannot will or work in First Church of Philippi, but God can. What a comfort it is to every pastor, knowing that God's work continues in our absence. And even when we're present, it's all still God's work.

God's work in
guarantees we work out.

Changing Our Story with God's Story

Just because we cannot see spiritual growth doesn't mean it's not there. If we are working on it, that means God is working on us, and God will work it out through our working out. Although the work is slower than we'd like, one of our greatest joys is seeing progress in holiness over time.

Summary: How do we keep working on holiness, when holiness doesn't seem to be working? *Keep working on your holiness because God keeps working on your holiness.*

Question: How can you add to your joy by seeing where God has added to your holiness?

Prayer: Worker, work in me, so that I can work for you. Awesome One, awe me so that I act for you.

Christian peace is worth fighting for.

16

The Bad Fight of Faith

PHILIPPIANS 2:14-16

I once watched a Ken Burns documentary series on World War II. After half a dozen episodes, I realized I was getting more and more depressed at the death and destruction I was watching. I was tempted to stop watching altogether, but decided instead that I would simply space the episodes out more so that I could preserve my mental health.

Why not permanently remove it from my watch list? Though difficult to watch, witnessing the horrors of war (even if just on a screen) can be a good thing. I believe we need to see the full consequences of war now if we are to avoid unnecessary wars in the future. Although not intended, the pictures and sounds of the suffering at Kabul airport have helped answer the question many have asked through the centuries: "How do we stop war?" Answer? "Show the catastrophic consequences."

Similarly, in Philippians 2:14-16, the apostle Paul uses the horrendous results of war as well as the happy results of peace to answer the question, *How do we stop church fights?*

Anticipate the Blessings of Peace 2:14-16

"Fight the good fight of the faith," Paul commanded Timothy (1 Tim. 6:12). Paul never flinched from a "good" fight. But some fights are bad fights. Such were the fights at First Church of Philippi. The Christians were fighting over minor matters, causing unnecessary division among them. Paul does not tell them to fight the good fight of faith, but to stop fighting bad fights of faithlessness. "Do all things without grumbling or disputing" (Phil. 2:14). Minimize your minor-league squabbles.

To motivate them, Paul connects happy consequences with a cease-fire. Notice particularly his "that you may be." "Do all things without grumbling or disputing, that you may be blameless and innocent, children of God without blemish in the midst of a crooked and twisted generation, among whom you shine as lights in the world, holding fast to the word of life, so that in the day of Christ I may be proud that I did not run in vain or labor in vain" (2:14–16).

Spiritually peaceful times are spiritually productive times. To paraphrase Paul, peace between Christians stops sin between Christians, builds assurance of our sonship, protects us from worldliness, brightens our witness, tightens our grip on the word of God, and encourages hardworking pastors.

Isn't that vision of peace and productivity appealing? Let's imagine the blessings of peace to make us long and work for a cease-fire.

Christian peace is worth fighting for.

And what if I don't?

Anticipate the Curses of Fighting 2:14–16

Although Paul doesn't spell it out explicitly, he clearly implies that if we do all things with grumbling and disputing, we'll see the opposite effects to peace and harmony. Christians who fight unnecessary fights will be blameworthy and guilty, they will lack assurance, they will be polluted by the world, they will deepen the darkness of our already dark world, they will lose their grip of the word, and they will discourage hardworking pastors. Paul shows the catastrophic consequences of unnecessary war to make them long for necessary peace. Let's fight the good fight of faith but surrender bad fights of faith.

If we fight over nothing, we'll lose everything.

Changing Our Story with God's Story

As I look back on my Christian life, I can see that I've moved from being a fast-fighter to more of a peacemaker. I hope it's not compromise, but rather the result of having lived through church fights and experienced some of the catastrophic consequences Paul warned about.

I've also seen the blessings of peace Paul promised, and therefore I'm more prepared to fight for peace than to fight for the sake of fighting. The day of Christ is coming, and I want to be ready for it myself as well as help others get ready for it.

Summary: How do we stop church fights? *Stop unnecessary church fights by anticipating the happy blessings of peace and the horrific curses of fighting.*

Question: In what ways have past church fights increased your fight for church peace?

Prayer: God of Peace, use me to spread Christian peace by making war against unnecessary Christian fighting.

Servants find satisfaction in service.

 Hear God's Story | Change Your Story | Tell the Story | Change Others' Stories

17

Satisfaction through Service

PHILIPPIANS 2:17-30

Where do you find satisfaction? What gives you pleasure and fulfillment? What makes you feel "in the zone"? You've tried many things, haven't you? So have I. Having tried multiple ways to find satisfaction, in my early twenties I ended up empty rather than filled, still asking the same question: *How can I find satisfaction?*

In Philippians 2:17-30, Paul stuns us with a surprising answer to that question. At first glance, these verses don't look too important. They seem to cover some personnel matters, with Paul arranging some substitutes for himself while he's in prison. But if we pause to dig into these words rather than skip over them, we discover that Paul is using even these staffing adjustments to teach the Philippians to find joyful satisfaction in unity and service.

I'm Willing to Serve You 2:17-18

Paul was willing "to be poured out as a drink offering upon the sacrificial offering of [the Philippian's] faith" (2:17). He viewed their faith as a sacrifice that he would complete by pouring out himself for them again. Nothing would make him happier than sacrificing himself in their service. As he put it, "I am glad and rejoice with you all. Likewise you also should be glad and rejoice with me" (2:17–18). The way to satisfaction is to satisfy others. The way to filling is emptying self to fill others.

Servants find satisfaction in service.

But what if Paul can't get out of prison to serve them again?
He'll send Timothy to serve them.

Timothy Will Serve You 2:19–24

Paul was planning to send Timothy to the Philippians to see how they were doing (2:19). He chose Timothy because, "I have no one like him, who will be genuinely concerned for your welfare. For they all seek their own interests, not those of Jesus Christ" (2:20–21). Timothy's service would be marked by selflessness for the sake of Christ. His own interests were neither urgent nor important, while others' interests were both urgent and important.

Paul's confidence in Timothy's future selfless service was based upon his past record of service. "But you know Timothy's proven worth, how as a son with a father he has served with me in the gospel" (2:22).

Servants serve others not themselves.

What else did the Philippians need
apart from servant-hearted Timothy?
Servant-hearted Epaphroditus.

Epaphroditus Will Serve You 2:25–30

Paul was hoping to visit, but, if not, he would send not only Timothy to the Philippians but also Epaphroditus, his "brother and fellow worker and fellow soldier, and your messenger and minister to [his] need" (2:25). Paul's description of Epaphroditus drives home the two areas he wanted the Philippians to work on: unity with one another and service of one another.

But hadn't Epaphroditus been sick? "Indeed he was ill, near to death" (2:27). But that didn't stop his service. "He nearly died for the work of Christ, risking his life to complete what was lacking in your service to me" (2:30). He would rather risk his life in his serving than risk a lack in the Philippians' serving. Epaphroditus's life was filled with giving, while the Philippians were full of taking.

Servants empty themselves to fill others.

Changing Our Story with God's Story

As we saw in chapter 13, Jesus emptied himself to serve others. That's what Jesus-followers do too. Like Jesus, we find pleasure in pouring, satisfaction in serving, and fulfillment in filling others. That kind of sacrificial service unites rather than divides and starts peace rather than war.

It's counterintuitive, but serving is more satisfying than being served. It's in our own interests to seek the interests of others. It's in our churches' interests to cultivate servants more than leaders.

Summary: How can I find satisfaction? *Find satisfaction in sacrificial and selfless service.*

Question: Who and how will you fill today?

Prayer: Satisfier, satisfy me by making me a satisfier of others. Fill me by making me pourable.

**All our happiness
is in Christ,
about Christ,
from Christ,
and for Christ.**

Hear
God's Story

Change
Your Story

Tell
the Story

Change
Others' Stories

18

Safe and Saving Happiness

PHILIPPIANS 3:1

I once wrote a book called *The Happy Christian*.[2] Many of my Christian friends and colleagues in the ministry viewed me as suspect when they heard about it. They thought I had embraced the prosperity gospel.

Another narrowed his eyes and asked, "What are you trying to do, David?"

"Make Christians happy!" I answered. You'd have thought I'd denied the resurrection.

How can I be happy? is one of the most fundamental human questions. It drives us. God allows us to answer it in a Christian way. In fact, he provides the Christian answer in Philippians 3:1.

Christian Joy Is Salvation Joy 3:1

For two chapters Paul has been hammering home *unity* and *truth*. Now he explains why. "Finally, my brothers, rejoice in the Lord" (3:1). His teaching about prioritizing unity through truth and truth through unity was driven by the motivation of securing maximal Christian joy for the miserable First Church of Philippi. Pride, lies, and division had depressed them. Humility, unity, and truth would elevate them.

---

2 David Murray, *The Happy Christian: Ten Ways to Be a Joyful Believer in a Gloomy World* (Nashville: Thomas Nelson, 2015).

Paul doesn't just say, "Rejoice!" or, "Be happy!" but, "Rejoice in the Lord! Be happy in the Lord!" The Lord he had just written so beautifully about was to be the spring and fountain of their joy.

As Christians we find our greatest joy in the Lord Jesus. We find happiness in who he is, was, and will be. We find happiness in what he did, does, and will do. We find happiness in what he said, says, and will say. We find happiness in his character, his conduct, and his communication. We find happiness in his words and actions. We find happiness in his beauty, grace, love, patience, gentleness, power, and sovereignty. We find happiness in his incarnation, crucifixion, resurrection, ascension, and reign. We find happiness in his word, his day, and his church. We find happiness in his creation, his providence, his salvation, his justification, his adoption, his sanctification, and his glorification.

All our happiness is in Christ,
about Christ, from Christ, and for Christ.

But is it okay to be so happy?

Christian Joy Is Safe Joy 3:1

There's a lot of dangerous happiness in the world. So many laughs are manufactured out of dirty language, people's pain, mockery, lies, and blasphemy. We laugh, but we know we should really cry. Such laughs are dangerous for the joker, the hearers, and the victims.

But Christian happiness is safe. "To write the same things to you is no trouble to me and is safe for you" (3:1). It damages no one and blesses everyone. It's good for the giver of joy, the receiver of joy, and the subject of joy.

Christian happiness is not only safe; it's saving. It is part of our salvation, helps our salvation, expresses our salvation, and communicates our salvation.

So why do some Christians view happiness with so much suspicion? Christian joy is safe joy. We can't get too much of it. It is safe and keeps us safe. Christian joy is an important emotional defense in a sadly dangerous world.

Christian joy is Christian security.

Changing Our Story with God's Story

Christ-centered joy is permanent, not passing. It's eternal, not ephemeral. It doesn't decline as we get older, but rather increases. It doesn't end when we die, but rather expands exponentially. It's one of our best apologetics for the faith, not something to apologize for. It's countercultural, but cultivates culture. No one is as happy as the happy Christian.

Summary: How can I be happy? *Rejoice in the Lord to express your salvation and keep you safe.*

Question: How do you find happiness in Jesus?

Prayer: Happy God, thank you for sharing your happiness and inviting me into it through Jesus.

Adding to Christ is subtracting from Christ.

19

Back to Basics

PHILIPPIANS 3:2–8

At family devotions, Shona will sometimes say, "David, I don't think Scot knows what that word means." Usually it's something I think is really basic and just assume that my eight–year-old understands. Shona is usually right, and I then try to explain the word or concept. And I usually learn in the process! Answering basic questions is helpful for everyone.

In Philippians 3:2–8, Paul answers the most basic question for the Philippians: What is a Christian? In other words, *How do I know if I'm a Christian?* Let's learn together with the Philippians as Paul goes back to basics to secure the Christian joy he spoke of in verse 1.

A Christian Puts No Confidence in the Flesh 3:2–6

Paul does not hold back when describing those who claimed to be Christians but were actually anti-Christian. "Look out for the dogs, look out for the evildoers, look out for those who mutilate the flesh" (3:2). Paul warns the Philippians to be on the lookout for anyone who insisted that circumcision was necessary for salvation. Treat them like dogs, Paul says. Put them out of the church as you would put a wild dog on the street. These self-proclaimed do-gooders were actually evildoers. After Christ, circumcision was no longer necessary. Indeed, it was self-mutilation.

Because of Christ, "we are the circumcision [meaning, we are God's true people] who worship by the Spirit of God and glory in Christ Jesus and put no confidence in the flesh" (3:3).

"No confidence in the flesh" means no confidence in self. If anyone had reason for self-confidence, it was Paul. "I myself have reason for confidence in the flesh also. If anyone else thinks he has reason for confidence in the flesh, I have more" (3:4). Paul had:

- *Religion:* "circumcised on the eighth day" (3:5)
- *Nationality:* "of the people of Israel" (3:5)
- *Tribe:* "of the tribe of Benjamin" (3:5)
- *Culture:* "a Hebrew of Hebrews" (3:5)
- *Morality:* "as to the law, a Pharisee" (3:5)
- *Activism:* "as to zeal, a persecutor of the church" (3:6)
- *Good works:* "as to righteousness under the law, blameless" (3:6)

Paul weighs all these reasons then says he puts zero confidence in any and all of them.

Savior-confidence replaces self-confidence.

So what is our confidence?

Christians Put Their Confidence in Christ 3:7–8

"Whatever gain I had," Paul says, "I counted as loss for the sake of Christ. Indeed, I count everything as loss because of the surpassing worth of knowing Christ Jesus my Lord" (3:7–8).

Paul had a ton of religious, family, and social capital. But once he discovered Christ, all these assets turned into liabilities on his balance sheet. His previous profits became losses. He therefore got rid of them all "because of the surpassing worth of knowing Christ Jesus my Lord" (3:8). Once Jesus became his prized asset, he saw everything else as negative and therefore put them in the trash. The more he saw his previous assets as garbage, the more he saw Christ as gain.

That's why he says, "We are the circumcision [God's true people], who worship by the Spirit of God and glory in Christ Jesus" (3:3). Christianity is not a rejection of circumcision and Judaism. It's the fulfillment of it. We no longer put our confidence in the flesh or in outward religion, but we worship by the Spirit and glory in Christ Jesus.

Adding to Christ is subtracting from Christ.

Changing Our Story with God's Story

We live in a world that prizes self-confidence. But if we want to live in the world to come, we must prize Christ-confidence and his reward. Getting back to basics is the only way forward. Getting the gospel right is the way to rejoice in the Lord.

Summary: How do I know if I'm a Christian? *Put zero confidence in the flesh and 100 percent confidence in Christ.*

Question: What do you count as a liability that you previously thought was an asset?

Prayer: Trustworthy Lord, drain my confidence in myself and build my confidence in you alone for gospel happiness.

Everything we lose for Christ is worth losing.

 Hear God's Story | Change Your Story | Tell the Story | Change Others' Stories

20

God Gives Gold for Garbage

PHILIPPIANS 3:8-11

I have found the number one reason people do not become Christians is the fear of what they will lose. I remember going through that calculation myself when the Lord was calling me to himself in my early twenties. I thought, "But I'll lose my job, my friends, my reputation, and my Sundays. Above all, I'll lose my sins, my sinful pleasures and habits." No matter how many times I tried to add things up, always hoping for a different answer, it always came out the same: too much to lose and too little to gain. So I resisted and resisted.

Thankfully, God helped me recalculate my losses, just as he did with the apostle Paul. Paul puts this better than I can in Philippians 3:8-11, where he addresses the question *What will I lose if I become a Christian?*

We Lose Garbage 3:8

Paul had just listed all he stood to lose by becoming a Christian, everything that could have given him confidence in self. We would expect that the cost would be too great. But instead, he says, "I count everything as loss because of the surpassing worth of knowing Christ Jesus my Lord" (3:8). What he once counted as assets, he now counts as liabilities. What changed? Christ entered the equation and turned all these profits into losses.

But Paul goes even further: "For his sake I have suffered the loss of all things and count them as rubbish, in order that I may gain Christ"

(3:8). He looks at all he used to value so highly and says, "Garbage! All of it is garbage." That's what we lose if we become a Christian. We lose garbage. It may not look like that now. That trash may look like gold. But it's fool's gold, a worthless stone that's fooling you into thinking it's precious gold.

Everything we lose for Christ is worth losing.

So what do I gain if I become a Christian?

We Gain Gold 3:8–10

What do we gain when we lose garbage? We gain gold. As Paul says, "I count everything as loss because of the surpassing worth of knowing Christ Jesus my Lord. For his sake I have suffered the loss of all things and count them as rubbish in order that I may gain Christ" (3:8).

What do we get when we get Christ? Paul adds it all up. We get united with Christ, we get the righteousness of Christ, we get the knowledge of Christ, we get the power of Christ, we get to suffer like Christ, we get to be like Christ, and we get to be resurrected by Christ (3:9–10).

Now that's gold worth finding and owning, isn't it? It's an infinite gold mine that we'll never stop digging into and in which we'll be forever finding new gold dust, gold nuggets, and gold bars.

Jesus Christ is the gold standard.

Changing Our Story with God's Story

We've valued gold more than God, we've pursued the world's millions rather than God's mercies, we've valued financial riches more than faith's riches, or we've invested in religion rather than in the Redeemer. Either way, we've been duped by the devil's Ponzi scheme. Let's therefore use this passage to cut our losses and transfer our hopes of eternal riches to our precious Savior, Jesus Christ. If you do, you'll discover as I did that you end up losing nothing and gaining everything.

Summary: What will I lose if I become a Christian? *Become a Christian because you will gain gold and lose garbage.*

Question: What did you give up for Christ or what will you give up for Christ?

Prayer: Treasurer, help me to find and value your gold and turn away from all fool's gold so that I can have an eternal retirement.

Don't pause on the plateau but press on to the peak.

21

Plateau, or Press to the Peak?

PHILIPPIANS 3:12–16

Forty years ago, I attended a mountain-climbing camp with my church. On the first day we tried to climb one of the highest mountains in the Scottish Highlands. It was especially tough because most of us city kids had never climbed a mountain before.

I still remember getting to what I thought was the peak only to realize that it was a plateau before the real peak. This was after hours of agonizing ascent. We were facing another hour of even harder climbing. Most of us decided enough was enough and that the flat plateau would be our peak. But a few kids, mostly country boys, used the plateau as an opportunity to rest and renew before pressing on to the real summit.

In every area of life (business, school, relationships, etc.), most people plateau, while a few press on to the summit. Most settle for mediocrity, but others refuse to settle and press on to peaks of excellence. It's the same in spiritual life. There are plateau Christians and there are peak Christians. *How can we make sure we are peak Christians rather than plateau Christians?* Let's join the apostle Paul as he climbs to the summit in Philippians 3:12–16.

We Press on to the Peak 3:12–14

Paul had attained to great heights in the Christian life: union with Christ, the righteousness of Christ, the knowledge of Christ, the power of Christ, suffering like Christ, becoming like Christ, and the hope of resurrection by Christ (3:9–10).

But then he says, "Not that I have already obtained this or am already perfect, but I press on to make it my own" (3:12). Most would have settled. Most would have plateaued and said, "That's high enough." Not Paul. He presses on to the peak. Instead of looking at all he had already climbed by God's grace, he turns to the plateau Christians and says, "Brothers, I do not consider that I have made it my own. But one thing I do: forgetting what lies behind and straining forward to what lies ahead, I press on toward the goal for the prize of the upward call of God in Christ Jesus" (3:13–14). He strains forward and pushes on, keeping the ultimate peak in view at all times.

Don't pause on the plateau
but press on to the peak.

"But I can't do this alone."
You don't have to.

Christ Pressed on to the Peak 3:12–16

One little phrase reminds us that we have a climbing partner: "I press on to make it my own, because Christ Jesus has made me his own" (3:12). This should probably be translated, "I press on to make *him* my own, because Christ Jesus has made me his own." Paul presses on for the prize of Christ because Christ pressed on for the prize of Paul. Paul pushes on through the pain barrier because Christ has already broken the pain barrier.

Paul used Christ's story to change his own and then urges the Philippians to do likewise: "Let those of us who are mature think this way, and if in anything you think otherwise, God will reveal that also to you. Only let us hold true to what we have attained" (3:15–16). We press on to Christ, for Christ, and with Christ.

We try because Christ triumphed.

Changing Our Story with God's Story

Every time Paul urges greater effort, he always brings in Christ as our energy source. Christless effort is doomed to plateau, but Christ-energized effort can climb Everest in triumph.

Summary: How can we make sure we are peak Christians rather than plateau Christians? *Use Christ as your Sherpa and press on to the peak of pleasure instead of plateauing in miserable mediocrity.*

Question: Where have you plateaued in your Christian life, and how can Christ help you press on to the peak?

Prayer: Magnificent Mountaineer, thank you for pushing through the pain barrier for me. Help me to push through the pain with you and for you so that I can have the joy of reaching the peak.

Copy Christ to be a copy-Christ, and one day you'll be a copy of Christ.

22

Copycat or Copy-Christ?

PHILIPPIANS 3:17-21

When I was a kid, it was an insult to be called a copycat. My school friends and I hurled this word around to mock anyone who copied someone's clothes, actions, or words.

But being a copycat isn't something we see just in children. Whether we like to admit it or not, we all copy someone to some degree. We're often unaware that we copy others, follow their example, and are influenced by them. They are our models; we are their mimics. That's fine when they're good examples, but disastrous when they're bad examples.

Paul saw this danger in Philippi. But instead of simply saying "stop copying others," he said "choose better models." "Brothers, join in imitating me, and keep your eyes on those who walk according to the example you have in us" (3:17). He sets himself up as a good model and warns about bad models. Paul's asking the Philippians and us, *Who is your model?*

Don't Copy Copycats 3:18-19

Paul was deeply grieved by the bad spiritual examples filling the vacuum left by his absence in Philippi. "For many, of whom I have often told you and now tell you even with tears, walk as enemies of the cross of Christ" (3:18).

How did Paul know they were bad examples? They are "enemies of the cross of Christ." They're not living a cross-shaped life but an

I-shaped life. They're not living a self-sacrificing lifestyle but a self-promoting lifestyle. "Their god is their belly, and they glory in their shame, with minds set on earthly things" (3:19). They live to satisfy their bodies, they boast in what they should be ashamed of, and they are living only for this earth's comforts and glories.

Therefore, "their end is destruction" (3:19). The bodies they pamper will perish. So don't look at their bloated, cosseted, overindulged bodies with envy but with sorrow.

No copycat has nine lives.

Whom should I copy?

Copy Copy-Christs 3:17, 20-21

"Brothers, join in imitating me, and keep your eyes on those who walk according to the example you have in us" (3:17). Copy me and those who copy me in Philippi. Paul is a copy of Christ, and therefore when he says, "Copy me," he's saying, "Copy copy-Christs."

Copy our citizenship. "Our citizenship is in heaven" (3:20). Our first interest, our greatest loyalty, and our highest concern is heaven.

Copy our waiting. "We await a Savior, the Lord Jesus Christ" (3:20). Our eyes are focused on heaven with longing for Jesus's appearance to save us from every remaining sin.

Copy our bodies. "[Jesus] will transform our lowly body to be like his glorious body, by the power that enables him even to subject all things to himself" (3:21). Give up your bodies to the Lord's service because the Lord will give you back a better body. Give up your power because Jesus will use his power over everything to transform everything about your body. Even though many parts of us continue to resist modeling Christlikeness, the day is coming when we will be perfectly moldable and perfectly molded.

Copy Christ to be a copy-Christ,
and one day you'll be a copy of Christ.

Changing Our Story with God's Story

It's impossible not to have a model. It's impossible not to be a model. The only questions are, Who is our model? and Whom am I modeling? Although *copycat* is a playground insult, *copy-Christ* is a praise, a privilege, and an honor. It's not a taunt to be avoided at all costs but a commendation to aspire to, whatever the cost.

Summary: Who is your model? *Find delight in copying those who sacrifice everything for Christ to gain everything from Christ.*

Question: How can you be a better copy-Christ?

Prayer: Perfect God, you are my perfect model. Use me as your imperfect model to point others to your perfection.

Personal peace is enjoyed in the castle of Christ.

23

Christ's Calming Castle

PHILIPPIANS 4:1-7

Causes cure. What do I mean by that? The first step to curing a problem is discovering the cause of the problem. For example, when I get flare-ups of arthritis, I can take pain relievers to tamp down the symptoms. But because I haven't addressed the cause of my flare-ups, as soon as I stop the pain relievers, my condition flares up again. Without knowing the cause, I don't really have a cure.

Most of the time, my arthritis flare-ups are caused by too much stress and too little sleep. When I admit that, and trace my pain to that, then I'm identifying the cause, and only then can I work toward a cure. In that sense, causes cure.

Think about anxiety. We can take meds to reduce the symptoms of anxiety, but it will almost always return when meds are stopped. So *how do we cure anxiety*? Identify the causes, as Paul does in Philippians 4:1-7.

Causes of Anxiety 4:1-5

Paul identifies some of the most common ingredients in the mix of anxiety.

Uncertainty creates instability inside and outside, which is why Paul says, "Therefore, my brothers, whom I love and long for, my joy and crown, stand firm in the Lord, my beloved" (4:1).

Conflict creates stress. Therefore, Paul says, "I entreat Euodia and I entreat Syntyche to agree in the Lord" (4:2).

Isolation creates loneliness. Therefore, says Paul, "I ask you also, true companion, help these women, who have labored side by side with me in the gospel together with Clement and the rest of my fellow workers, whose names are in the book of life" (4:3).

Sadness creates depression. Therefore, Paul exhorts, "Rejoice in the Lord always; again I will say, rejoice" (4:4).

Anger creates tension. Therefore, Paul calms with, "Let your reasonableness be known to everyone" (4:5).

What a horrible mix: uncertainty and instability, conflict and stress, isolation and loneliness, sadness and depression, anger and tension. No wonder anxiety results from baking all of this in our heart ovens.

Poisonous ingredients will poison our insides.

What's the cure?

Three Cures for Anxiety 4:5-7

Paul calls us to throw out the previous ingredients and replace them with three new ingredients.

The first is the presence of the Lord. "The Lord is at hand" (4:5). Remember that the Lord is near, right beside us, no farther away than our hand.

Second is prayer. "Do not be anxious about anything, but in everything by prayer and supplication with thanksgiving let your requests be made known to God" (4:6). Instead of talking to ourselves and others, let's talk to God about everything we need, remembering to thank God for everything we already have.

Third is the peace of God. "And the peace of God, which surpasses all understanding, will guard your hearts and your minds in Christ Jesus" (4:7). The presence of God plus prayer to God results in the peace of God.

As Paul bakes this new cake, he finds a strange, surreal, inexplicable, mysterious calm comes over him. His heart and mind are no longer assailed and assaulted but garrisoned and guarded by the castle of Christ.

Personal peace is enjoyed in the castle of Christ.

Changing Our Story with God's Story

Some anxiety has a physical cause, and is the result of a disordered stress response system in our bodies. In that case, a doctor should be involved; physical remedies, including medication, may be required. However, where anxiety has a spiritual cause, it needs a spiritual cure. Thankfully, we have a great physician in Jesus Christ, who loves to say to us, "Peace! Be still!" (Mark 4:39).

Summary: How do we cure anxiety? *Mix God's presence, prayer, and peace to bake the cake of Christ-centered calm.*

Question: What's causing your anxiety, and how will you cure it?

Prayer: God of Peace, I confess my unnecessary anxiety and what causes it. Secure my heart with your presence, prayer, and peace.

God in,
good out.

24

God in, Good Out

PHILIPPIANS 4:8-9

Scientists estimate that for every hundred pieces of information that enter our brains, ninety-nine end up in the spam folder. Noticing only one thing out of every hundred is a good thing. As many people who have autism will tell you, if you don't have a good mental spam filter, you can be overwhelmed with useless and harmful data.

The problem is, many of us have spam filters that are fantastic at letting in only the negative things and filtering out the positive. With such a grim input of one-sided data, is it any wonder that we experience so much stress, demotivation, and relational breakdown?

How do we develop a better spam filter in our minds? In Philippians 4:8–9, Paul retrains our brains and SPAM filters so that we Scan for Positive and Affirming Messages.

Eat Feast Food, Not Fast Food 4:8-9

We can, and should, feed our minds a media diet that is biased toward what is good and beautiful. Here's Paul's diet.

His appetizer is "whatever is true." Avoid listening to lies, misrepresentation, imbalance, and distortion. Seek out the most truthful, balanced, and fair reporting of what's going on in the world.

His drink is "whatever is honorable." Trash the tawdry and nourish the noble in your life. Seek out and consume media that elevate the heroic, that inspire awe, and that generate worship.

His main course is "whatever is just." Seek out and celebrate right behavior: stories of hardworking parents, loving fathers, devoted mothers, respectful children, and so on.

His dessert is "whatever is pure." Grow a more positive mindset by taking extra time to think about the positives and allowing them to sink in.

His beverage is "whatever is lovely." Drink in what is beautiful, attractive, admirable, and winsome.

His favorite coffee is "whatever is commendable." Feast on whatever makes people exclaim, "Well done!" rather than what makes them say, "That's terrible."

Here's Paul's five-star review: "If there is any excellence, if there is anything worthy of praise, think about these things" (4:8).

This wasn't just a theory for Paul; he could appeal to the people's memory of him: "What you have learned and received and heard and seen in me—practice these things" (4:9).

This takes huge mental effort. It's not some kind of laid-back, freewheeling, blue-sky thinking. It requires concentration and focus on these subjects until we develop new thinking habits.

A good SPAM filter will reject bad SPAM food.

What are the health benefits?

Enjoy Peace, Not Panic 4:9

Paul promises long-term health benefits from this kind of media diet. "The God of peace will be with you" (4:9). Just as the quality of the food we put in our mouths affects our thinking, feeling, and doing, so the kinds of words, sounds, and images we put in our ears and eyes will have the same effect. Garbage in, garbage out.

On the other hand, if we starve ourselves of mental junk and replace it with what is true, admirable, right, pure, beautiful, and attractive, peace will stand as a sentinel all around our feelings and thoughts, creating an impregnable fortress of calm and tranquility. The peace of God and the God of peace will be with you.

God in, good out.

Changing Our Story with God's Story

If we let what is false, offensive, dishonest, filthy, ugly, and loathsome into our minds, we might as well sign up for a course on how to be hyperanxious. These interlopers drive peace from the castle, lower the drawbridge, and invite the armies of worry and instability into our mental citadel. Change your story by changing your diet.

Summary: How do we develop a better SPAM filter? *Choose a deliberate imbalance in favor of what is inspirational and wholesome, and you'll enjoy peace and joy.*

Question: How will you change your media diet to experience true peace and joy?

Prayer: True God of Truth, remove all falsehood and junk media from my life and replace them with what is true and wholesome so that I can enjoy your peace and joy.

The school of contentment has few students and even fewer graduates.

Hear
God's Story

Change
Your Story

Tell
the Story

Change
Others' Stories

25

The School of Contentment

PHILIPPIANS 4:10–13

Which is harder: contentment when poor or contentment when rich? Most of us would say it's much harder to be content when poor. "If only the Lord would give me this income, this house, this car, this retirement, then I would find it easy to be content."

In Philippians 4:10–13, the apostle Paul surprises us by saying that we have to learn how to be content whether we are rich or poor. Contentment does not rise or fall with our incomes and mutual funds. It rises and falls based on our spiritual condition. *How can we learn contentment?*

We Can Be Content When Poor 4:10–12

Paul had passed through a time of poverty and need, and the Philippians had eventually stepped in to mitigate his poverty and supply his need. "I rejoiced in the Lord greatly that now at length you have revived your concern for me. You were indeed concerned for me, but you had no opportunity" (4:10).

While rejoicing in God's reviving of their concern for Paul and their supplying what he lacked, Paul is careful to remind them that his contentment was not dependent on having money. "Not that I am speaking of being in need, for I have learned in whatever situation I am to be content" (4:11). Specifically, he learned "how to be brought low, and . . . the secret of facing plenty and hunger, abundance and need" (4:12).

Contentment in poverty is a state of mind and heart that accepts whatever financial situation we are in as God's plan for us at that time. Positively, it means being satisfied with what we have as God's wise plan for us. Negatively, it means we are not to envy others to whom God has given more.

This did not come easy to Paul. He had to learn it. He had many tough days in this school where he probably failed some tests and exams, but he finally graduated with honors.

The school of contentment has few students and even fewer graduates.

But I'd be content if only I had a bit more.

We Can Be Content When Rich 4:10–12

Paul had also known good times. But they didn't make contentment any easier. He had to learn contentment not only when he had little but also when he had lots. "I have learned in whatever situation I am to be content." Some find the "Rich and Content" class even harder than the "Poor and Content" class. Paul learned in both and passed both. "I know how to be brought low, and I know how to abound. In any and every circumstance, I have learned the secret of facing plenty and hunger, abundance and need" (4:12).

Few people are poor and content, but even fewer are rich and content.

Changing Our Story with God's Story

If you're poor, you're probably asking, "How did Paul learn this?" If you're rich, you're probably asking, "How did Paul learn this?" We go back to our original question: *How can we learn contentment?*

Paul closes this section by pointing us to his teacher and giving him all the credit: "I can do all things through him who strengthens me" (4:13). When Paul found his contentment muscle weakening, he called in his trainer, Jesus Christ, to strengthen him. Christ powered Paul's satisfaction and weakened his envy by saying to him, "Paul, if you have me, you have everything. I am what you need most and I can supply all your needs." Find spiritual contentment, and you'll find it much easier to find financial contentment.

Summary: How can I learn contentment? *Learn cheerful contentment through learning cheer in Christ.*

Question: What exercise or experience has helped you learn contentment?

Prayer: Teacher, I confess I forget a lot of what I learn in the contentment class. Make me a better student so that, whether rich or poor, I can pass the class with joy.

God's giving
gives him glory.

26

The Checkbook of the Bank of Faith

PHILIPPIANS 4:14-20

At some point in our lives, most of us experience some degree of financial need. I have had a few serious financial worries over the course of my life. The first was when I lost a lot of money on a business venture in my early twenties. The second was when I was a student for the ministry, and I was working as a delivery driver to make ends meet. The third was when I went nine months without a call to serve a church. *How will I survive?* I kept worrying.

These were horrible months full of fear, anxiety, and stress. But one day, while browsing a used bookstore, I came across a little book by Charles Spurgeon, *Chequebook of the Bank of Faith*. It contained daily readings based on Philippians 4:19. The ten cents I paid for that little book was one of the best investments I ever made. It brought me much peace and calm. Let's look at this verse in its context.

God Loves Givers 4:14-18

Paul had low times in his life and ministry when he was poor and hungry (4:12). One of those times, he tells the Philippians, was "in the beginning of the gospel, when I left Macedonia, no church entered into partnership with me in giving and receiving, except you only. Even in Thessalonica you sent me help for my needs once and again" (4:15–16). "It was kind of you to share my trouble" (4:14).

When Paul received the Philippians' financial support, his first thought was not, "Great! Now I have some money." It was, "Great!

The Philippians are producing fruit that will help them when they have to give account on the judgment day." "Not that I seek the gift, but I seek the fruit that increases to your credit" (4:17).

More recently, the Philippians gave again. They gave so much that Paul says, "I have received full payment, and more. I am well supplied, having received from Epaphroditus the gifts you sent" (4:18). Paul is delighted, but so is God. Their gift is "a fragrant offering, a sacrifice acceptable and pleasing to God" (4:18).

God delights in our donations.

Does God simply watch giving with pleasure?
No, he is behind all giving.
They gave to Paul because God gave to them.

God Loves Giving 4:19–20

Sometimes God supplies our needs directly. Other times, as here, he supplies our needs indirectly through his people. But whether direct or indirect, it is all ultimately from God.

Just in case the Philippians worried that their giving would leave them short, Paul assures them that "my God will supply every need of yours according to his riches in glory in Christ Jesus" (4:19). They had no need to fear any financial shortage because God was their bank, heaven was their vault, and Jesus was their cashier.

God loves to go to his "riches in glory" bank every day to distribute his resources to his people. He gives extravagantly to some, but meets the needs of all. Every day he issues checks in Jesus's name to each of his people. The amount is "every need supplied." God loves giving. No wonder Paul concludes his letter with, "To our God and Father be glory forever and ever. Amen" (4:20).

God's giving gives him glory.

Changing Our Story with God's Story

The Bank of Faith has full vaults for every needy sinner. It's a bank for the bankrupt and will never go bankrupt. It welcomes those with the worst credit and turns them from sad receivers into glad givers.

Summary: How will I survive? *God loves supplying my needs, and therefore I will enjoy supplying the needs of others, knowing that both methods give God and us pleasure.*

Question: How has God supplied your needs so you can supply the needs of others?

Prayer: Giver of Every Good and Perfect Gift, use me to model your cheerful giving so others turn to the giver.

COLOSSIANS

Don't just hope for change, but use hope to change yourself, your church, and your world.

27

Heavenly Hope or Worldly Pessimism?

COLOSSIANS 1:1–8

Should we be more pessimistic? Believe it or not, the *New York Times* asked that question in 2020, one of the darkest years in recent history. It was hard to be more pessimistic than we already were, yet the writer argued for the benefits of more pessimism.[3]

The apostle Paul would never have written such an article. He saw that pessimism was threatening the health of the young church at Colossae, and he wrote them a letter to motivate and move them toward heavenly hope.

How do we move from being worldly pessimists to being heavenly hopers? Let's see how Paul launched the Colossians along this trajectory in Colossians 1:1–8.

Heavenly Hope Is Thankful 1:3–5

Paul thanks God for the Colossians' faith and love, tracing these beautiful graces to the sovereign grace of God alone. "We always thank God, the Father of our Lord Jesus Christ, when we pray for you, since we heard of your faith in Christ Jesus and of the love that you have for all the saints" (1:3–4).

---

3 Reggie Ugwu, "Should We Be More Pessimistic?," *New York Times*, June 17, 2020, www.nytimes.com.

Paul also thanks God for the Colossians' heavenly hope. "We thank God . . . because of the hope laid up for you in heaven" (1:4–5). Hope can be objective (what we hope for) or subjective (the feeling of hope). Each multiplies the other. Here Paul focuses the Colossians on the objective, the hope "laid up for them in heaven" (1:5), knowing that the fact of their hope will increase their feeling of hope.

Worldly pessimism will drag us down in discontent,
but heavenly hope will lift us up with gratitude.

Is this hope all heavenly and future or
is it of any practical use on this earth?

Heavenly Hope Is Productive 1:4–6

Heavenly hope produces present fruit in individuals. The Colossians have faith and love "because of the hope" (1:5). The NIV says their faith in Christ and love for the saints "spring from the hope that is stored up for you in heaven." Hope sustains, renews, revitalizes, and stimulates ongoing faith and love. Because we increasingly know how many blessings are reserved for us in heaven, that growing hope continually fertilizes our faith and love.

Heavenly hope also produces fruit in the church. The specific fruit mentioned is their "love in the Spirit" (1:8). Heavenly hope drives pessimism and hatred out of the Christian community and cultivates love and fellowship.

Don't just hope for change,
but use hope to change yourself,
your church, and your world.

How do I get this productive hope?

Heavenly Hope Is Announced in the Gospel 1:5–8

So how do we get and increase this hope? The Colossians "heard . . . the word of the truth, the gospel" (1:5). They "heard it and understood the grace of God in truth" (1:6). If we want to get hope and increase hope, we must hear the gospel more and believe the gospel more. This is true hope not false hope, real hope not pretend hope, factual hope not fictional hope.

Be obsessed with the good news of the Bible,
not the bad news of the media.

Changing Our Story with God's Story

Pessimism drains gratitude, pessimism is barren, and pessimism is obsessed with bad news. Heavenly hope causes thanksgiving, is productive, and is obsessed with the gospel. Heavenly hope is true hope. Heavenly hope is happy hope. Heavenly hope is fruitful hope. Heavenly hope is transformative hope. Heavenly hope is gospel hope. Let's therefore ask the God of hope to make us more hope-full by making us more gospel-full.

Summary: How do we move from being a worldly pessimist to being a heavenly hoper? *Get and grow in gospel-fertilized heavenly hope to increase fruitfulness, gratitude, and hope.*

Question: How can you change your identity from pessimist or optimist to hope-ist?

Prayer: My Hope, thank you for unblocking the pipeline of productive gospel hope, changing my identity from an Eeyore to a Tigger.

People-pleasing drains us, but God-pleasing strengthens us.

28

From People-Pleasing to God-Pleasing

COLOSSIANS 1:9-14

Trying to make other people happy is guaranteed to make us unhappy. It's impossible to please everyone all the time, and trying to can make us sin, which makes God unhappy too. So at the end of the day, we're unhappy, people are unhappy, and God is unhappy. *How do we stop trying to be people-pleasers and therefore nobody-pleasers?*

Paul was asking this question because the Colossian church had come under the influence of false teachers (the Gnostics/Know-It-Alls), and the infant Colossian Christians were trying to please them instead of God. In Colossians 1:9-14, Paul shows them four ways to change from being people-pleasers to being God-pleasers.

Increased Fruitfulness Pleases God 1:10

Paul prayed that the Colossians would "walk in a manner worthy of the Lord, fully pleasing to him: bearing fruit in every good work" (1:10). The Gnostics (Know-It-Alls), said, "It doesn't matter how you live. All that matters is what you know." The apostle pushed back: "No, there must be fruit; there must be good works too." God is pleased with good fruit. Good fruit makes God a happy gardener.

People-pleasing produces rotten fruit and an angry God,
but God-pleasing produces good fruit and a happy God.

I love the idea of producing fruit to please God,
but how do I know what pleases him?

Increased Theology Pleases God 1:10

Paul prayed that they would please God by "increasing in the knowledge of God" (1:10). Just because the Know-It-Alls were making knowledge everything, Paul did not make it nothing. Also, contrary to the Know-It-Alls, who reserved the highest knowledge for just the elite, Paul prayed that every Colossian believer would know God more through his word.

People-pleasing depends on mind reading.
God-pleasing depends on Bible-reading.

More fruit and more theology? How can I ever do that?

Increased Dependence Pleases God 1:11

The third way they could please God was by "being strengthened with all power, according to his glorious might, for all endurance and patience with joy" (1:11). How do we get God's power? Active dependence. We are to actively rely on God's power because God empowers the powerless who seek his power. We know so little of God's nuclear power because we rely so much on our own AAA battery power.

The result of this active dependence is that God strengthens "for all endurance and patience with joy" (1:11). We need divine power just to stand still. Standing still by God's strength is more pleasing to him than making great strides in our own strength!

People-pleasing drains us, but God-pleasing strengthens us.

God gives me his glorious power to endure
joyfully to the end. How can I repay?

Increased Thanks Pleases God 1:12–14

Paul prayed that they would please God by "giving thanks to the Father, who has qualified you to share in the inheritance of the saints in light" (1:12). Although we were disqualified from heaven, God the Father qualifies us by accepting Christ's qualifications on our behalf. And if he qualifies us, no one can disqualify us.

What else do we get to give thanks for? "He has delivered us from the domain of darkness and transferred us to the kingdom of his beloved Son, in whom we have redemption, the forgiveness of sins" (1:13–14). We've been transported from one world to another, from a world of darkness to a world of love, and have been bought back from the slavery of sin by the forgiveness of sins.

People-pleasing produces bitterness,
but God-pleasing results from thanksgiving.

Changing Our Story with God's Story

People-pleasing is our default identity, but God-pleasing is our deluxe identity. No one pleased God better than Jesus, which is why God said, "With [him] I am well pleased" (Matt. 3:17). We please God most when we're pleased with Christ most.

Summary: How do we stop the people-pleasing that pleases nobody? *Live to please God through increased fruitfulness, theology, dependence, and gratitude.*

Question: How will you use this text to change your identity from people-pleaser to God-pleaser?

Prayer: All-Wise God, fill me with spiritual wisdom so that I can please you with increased fruitfulness, theology, dependence, and gratitude and so change my identity to a God-pleaser.

Christ will not be supreme in our hearts if the church is not supreme in our lives.

 Hear God's Story | Change Your Story | Tell the Story | Change Others' Stories

29

Restoring the Supremacy of Christ to Our Worldview

COLOSSIANS 1:15–20

When you view the world, what stands out as first and foremost? Is it a global pandemic? A world leader? Or is the Lord Jesus first and most? I've found that when Christ is not supreme in my worldview, I end up with a wrong view of the world and of Christ.

How do we restore the supremacy of Christ to our worldview? Let's look at how Paul helped the Colossians recover the supremacy of Christ, so that we can get help too.

Christ Is Supreme in the First Creation 1:15–17

Paul lifts up Christ's supremacy in the creation of the world with five truths.

Christ is "the image of the invisible God" (1:15). As the image of God, Christ is the one who makes the invisible visible, who makes the unknowable knowable.

Christ is "the firstborn of all creation" (1:15). In the Colossian context, "firstborn" is not about time but about place. It's not chronological but geographical. It means Christ is over all creation.

Christ is the Creator of all things (1:16). Why does he have primacy and authority over all creatures? Because he is the Creator of them all. He is the uncreated Creator of all. "All things were created through him and for him" (1:16). Just as all creation went out from him, so all creation is for him.

Christ is "before all things, and in him all things hold together" (1:17). Christ did not simply make everything and then walk away from his creation. He continues to hold it all together.

If Christ is not first and most in our world,
then we are last and lost in the world.

But the first creation is broken and dysfunctional.
Can Christ do anything about that?

Christ Is Supreme in the Re-Creation 1:18

Christ is recreating this broken world through the church. As such, "he is the head of the body, the church" (1:18). Just as Christ, the head of creation, created humanity in the world, so Christ, the head of the church, is recreating humanity in the church.

Christ is also the life of the church. "He is the beginning, the firstborn from the dead" (1:18). Christ's resurrection was the first real resurrection in that he rose never to die again. The power of his resurrection flows into the church.

The aim of this re-creation is "that in everything he might be preeminent" (1:18). Christ will have the first place in all things through having first place in the church.

Christ will not be supreme in our hearts
if the church is not supreme in our lives.

But the church is also broken and dysfunctional.
Can Christ do anything about that?

Christ Is Supreme in the New Creation 1:19–20

Christ's supremacy will be seen most clearly in the new creation—the new heaven and the new earth. There we will fully see Christ as the fullness of God (1:19) and as the reconciler to God (1:20). This ruptured and divided creation will be repaired and recreated through the blood of Christ's cross so that not one part of Christ's new creation will be opposed to him.

The best on this earth is emptiness and nothingness,
but Christ in heaven is fullness and enoughness.

Changing Our Story with God's Story

A fuller view of Christ will give us a better view of this world and the next. When we see Christ clearer, we see everything clearer. Thankfully, this kind of eyesight doesn't fade with age but sees further with faith.

Summary: How do we restore the supremacy of Christ to our worldview? *Live for Christ as supreme over all time and places to increase Christ-awareness on earth, Christ-worship in the church, and Christ-hope in heaven.*

Question: What difference will this view of Christ make to your view of this world and the world to come?

Prayer: Creator, give me a right view of Christ so that I get a right view of this world and the world to come.

Our fear of falling destabilizes us, but Christ's call to persevere secures us.

30

Gospel Motives for Gospel Perseverance

COLOSSIANS 1:21–23

We're living in times of increasing opposition to the gospel: verbal opposition, economic opposition, workplace opposition, legal opposition, and so on. Many have given up part of the faith, especially in the area of sexual ethics. Some have given up all of the faith and abandoned the gospel altogether. Some have been well-known Christian leaders. No wonder we sometimes ask ourselves, *How can I persevere when I am so weak and the opposition is so strong?*

In Colossians 1:21–23 Paul strengthens us with three truths that remove this destabilizing fear and replace it with a confident expectation of perseverance.

Christ Has Made Peace for You 1:21–22

Paul reminds the Colossians what they once were: "Alienated and hostile in mind, doing evil deeds" (1:21). They were strangers and enemies, consumed by their evil thoughts about God and evil actions against God.

But God did not leave them in spiritual alienation and aggression: "He has now reconciled [us] in his body of flesh by his death" (1:22). They were active in alienation and aggression but passive in reconciliation. Christ took them over to God's side and God over to their side by taking away sin. Their evil works produced an alienated life. Christ's body produced a reconciled life.

Gospel opposition turns our focus to people,
but gospel peace turns our focus to Christ.

Remembering the past does encourage perseverance.
But what lies ahead?

Christ Will Make You Perfect 1:22

What's the aim of Christ's reconciliation? It is "in order to present you holy and blameless and above reproach before him" (1:22). He's aiming at a presentation of perfection.

Everything Christ did on Easter Friday was with a view to judgment day, the day when he will make the most incredible presentation of imperfect sinners as perfect saints. This future is so certain that we can rejoice in the present. It's like having been treated for a painful snake bite and waiting with confident joy for the antidote to work.

Present gospel opposition can demoralize us,
but future gospel perfection motivates us.

I've looked to the past, and I've looked to the future.
What do I do in the present?

Christ Calls You to Persevere 1:23

All this will be ours *if*: "If indeed you continue in the faith, stable and steadfast, not shifting from the hope of the gospel that you heard" (1:23).

Based on these two truths—Christ has made peace and Christ will perfect—Paul calls the Colossians to "continue in the faith." They will not continue in faith (subjective) unless they continue in the faith (objective). If they lose *the* faith, they will lose *their* faith.

But if they continue in the faith, they will be "stable and steadfast." *Stable* describes the firmness of the foundation, *steadfast* the firmness of their grip on the foundation. Believers need good ground and a good grip. But they also need good grit. "Not shifting from the hope of the gospel" is a determination to hold on to the hope of the gospel, whatever the opposition.

Our fear of falling destabilizes us,
but Christ's call to persevere secures us.

Changing Our Story with God's Story

There is no better preservative than the gospel. Nothing sustains gospel faith like faith in the gospel. Daily faith in Christ preserves us until the day of Christ. We don't need to do extraordinary things; just believe these extraordinary truths—Christ has made peace and Christ will make us perfect—and we will have extraordinary preservation.

Summary: How can I persevere when I am so weak and the opposition is so strong? *Persevere in faith and hope because Christ has made peace for us and will make us perfect.*

Question: How will you change your identity from at-risk to secure with this passage?

Prayer: Preserver, give me gospel perseverance through gospel peace and gospel perfection.

Culture-shaped service is hope in you, but Bible-shaped hope is Christ in you.

31

The Danger of Culture-Shaped Gospel Service

COLOSSIANS 1:24–29

Is our Christian service Bible-shaped or culture-shaped? When we are shaped by the culture more than by the word of God, we will have wrong expectations, the wrong message, the wrong aims, and the wrong power source. So *what does Bible-shaped gospel service look like?* The apostle Paul supplies a job description of gospel service in Colossians 1:24–29.

A Gospel Servant Suffers Like Christ 1:24

Paul expected that gospel service would produce gospel suffering: "Now I rejoice in my sufferings for your sake, and in my flesh I am filling up what is lacking in Christ's afflictions for the sake of his body, that is, the church" (1:24). Aware that the Colossians could no longer see Christ's in-person suffering, Paul stands in the gap and fills Christ's place with a visible demonstration of what Christ suffered out of love for his church. He doesn't just tell of Christ's sufferings; he embodies them.

That's why Paul can say, "I rejoice in my sufferings for your sake." He does not rejoice in his sufferings *per se*; he rejoices in them because of whom they exhibit (Jesus) and whom they benefit (the church).

Culture-shaped service rejoices in comfort,
but Bible-shaped service rejoices in suffering.

That doesn't sound like a very attractive job description.
Any positives?

A Gospel Servant Speaks the Hope of Christ 1:25-27

God commissioned Paul and gave him a stewardship, a responsibility to "make the word of God fully known" (1:25). As Paul did so, "the mystery hidden for ages and generations [has been] revealed to his saints" (1:26). This mystery is unveiled in two stages: first, Christ is *for* the Gentiles, and second, Christ is *in* the Gentiles. The gospel is not just revealed to a much wider audience (Jews and Gentiles); it's revealed in much greater depth and detail. It is "Christ in you, the hope of glory" (1:27).

Culture-shaped service is hope in you,
but Bible-shaped hope is Christ in you.

Speaking of this hope is an immense honor.
But what does it accomplish?

A Gospel Servant Aims at Likeness to Christ 1:28

The gospel servant preaches Christ as widely as possible, "warning everyone and teaching everyone with all wisdom" (1:28). It's always Christ-centered, but the tone and temperature vary depending on the audience, sometimes warning, sometimes teaching.

Whatever tone or method is used, the aim is always the same. It's not popularity or numbers; it's "that we may present everyone mature in Christ" (1:28).

Culture-shaped service aims at cultural norms,
but Bible-shaped service aims at Christlikeness.

The expectation is suffering, the message is Christ,
and the aim is Christ's likeness. How can I ever accomplish this?

A Gospel Servant Serves by the Power of Christ 1:29

Paul realizes this is no easy task, but that realization doesn't make him give up. Instead, it makes him "toil, struggling with all [Christ's] energy" (1:29). The end is so great that it's worth giving his all to it.

But he doesn't rely on the strength of his own effort. He strenuously contends "with all [Christ's] energy that he powerfully works within me" (1:29). The best test of whether we are working in our own strength or Christ's is asking ourselves this question: How much do we pray?

Culture-shaped service is self-powered,
but Bible-shaped service is Christ-powered.

Changing Our Story with God's Story

Every time we engage in gospel service, two very different molds battle to shape us: one from the world and one from God's word. They battle to impose different identities, expectations, messages, aims, and power sources, and therefore produce very different outcomes.

Summary: In a world of so many cultural pressures, what does Bible-shaped gospel service look like? *Shape the culture with a Bible-shaped identity that serves like Christ, for Christ, and by Christ.*

Question: How did this passage reshape how you see yourself and how you serve?

Prayer: Perfect Potter, I've been misshaped by the culture, therefore reshape me with the gospel so that I serve Christ like Christ, for Christ, and by Christ.

Scammers attack loveless and divided Christians, but Christian love unites and defends Christians.

32

Two Defenses against Scammers

COLOSSIANS 2:1-5

From time to time, I hear and read warnings about scammers in my area. The police or consumer protection groups alert the public to the danger, tell us what to look out for, and teach us how to avoid being scammed.

But spiritual scamming is much more widespread and much more dangerous. Many have been taken in and taken away by various spiritual errors in doctrine, worship, and practice. *How do we avoid being scammed?*

In Colossians 2:1–5, the apostle Paul provides us with two preemptive measures that can defend us from spiritual scammers. Some spiritual scammers (the Know-It-All Gnostics) had infiltrated the Colossian church. Paul already buttressed the Colossians with the gospel in chapter 1; in chapter 2 he adds two further lines of defense.

Christian Love Defends Us 2:1-2

Paul was in a great struggle for the Colossians. He was fighting for their faith, giving his all for their survival. His first line of defense was Christian love. He fought "that their hearts may be encouraged, being knit together in love" (2:2).

We are strengthened in heart by love in our hearts. *Knit* here can be literally translated "welded." Love welds people together. When believers stand shoulder to shoulder rather than as isolated or divided individuals, they are much stronger.

Scammers attack loveless and divided Christians, but Christian love unites and defends Christians.

"Is love for one another enough to protect me from scamming?"
No, but it's the essential foundation for what will: knowing Christ's riches.

Christian Knowledge Defends Us 2:2-3

Having defended with Christian love, the second line of defense is Christian knowledge. Paul fights to ensure that the Colossians "reach all the riches of full assurance of understanding and the knowledge of God's mystery, which is Christ, in whom are hidden all the treasures of wisdom and knowledge" (2:2-3). Paul doesn't contrast love with knowledge. Knowledge of God produces love, and love produces knowledge of God.

This is full knowledge. "*All* the riches of *full* assurance of understanding" (2:2). There is nothing lacking in the knowledge of Christ. Christians are already full and don't need the "higher knowledge" the Gnostics offered.

This is confident knowledge. "The full *assurance* of understanding" (2:2). When it comes to God and the gospel, doubt is dangerous and certainty is safe.

This is hidden knowledge. "In [Christ] are *hidden* all the treasures of wisdom and knowledge" (2:3). *Hidden* implies that it takes some effort to find, that such knowledge will not be found by half-hearted students. But Paul gives them a huge clue: it's hidden in Christ.

This is rich knowledge. "In whom are hidden all the *treasures* of wisdom and knowledge" (2:3). If you dig up this knowledge, you will value it higher than anything else in your life.

This is vast knowledge. "In whom are hidden *all* the treasures of wisdom and knowledge" (2:3). Everything you can possibly need is in Christ. If all you know is Christ, you have all you need to know. Nothing extra is required. Faith in Christ is the key to all of God's treasures. He is the only way to access the wisdom and knowledge of God.

Scammers thrive in ignorance,
but knowing Christ defends the soul.

Changing Our Story with God's Story

I was duped once into buying a training course on Facebook that promised much and delivered next to nothing. I was annoyed with myself because I lost over a hundred dollars. But spiritual scamming is far more dangerous and damaging. Let's use the Colossians' experience to protect not only our money but our souls.

Summary: How do we avoid being scammed? *Defend yourself from spiritual scamming with the treasures of Christian love and Christian knowledge, so that you are a victor not a victim.*

Question: How will you build your spiritual defenses today so that you do not become a victim of scammers?

Prayer: God of Truth, defend me from spiritual deception by increasing love for your people and for your truth.

Christology is not an optional extra but a source of safety and maturity.

33

Welcoming and Walking with Jesus

COLOSSIANS 2:6-7

One of my daughters has type 1 diabetes. Her regular clinic visits always focus on one number, her HbA1c. The lower the better. If it's lower, the medical staff ask her, "What did you do differently to make this improvement?" The basic idea is, "Whatever you've been doing, let's keep doing it. As you've begun, so continue."

The same idea applies to progress in our spiritual lives. When we ask, *How do I go forward in the Christian life?* Paul points backward in Colossians 2:6-7 to how we began and says, "Continue as you began." So what did our beginning look like?

We Welcomed Jesus 2:6

"Therefore, as you received Christ Jesus the Lord . . ." (2:6). The word *received* here is used to describe the welcoming of a person.

The Colossians welcomed this person as *Christ*, the Greek word for *Messiah*, or the one whom God anointed to be our prophet, priest, and king.

They welcomed him as *Jesus*, the personal name given to Christ when he became man, and which means "Savior."

They welcomed him as *Lord*, the one who ascended to heaven's throne and has universal authority over our lives. They welcomed him as Christ, Jesus, and Lord.

We welcome Jesus
because he first welcomed us.

"So, if that's how we welcomed Jesus,
how do we walk with Jesus?"
Exactly the same way!

We Walk in Jesus 2:6–7

"... so walk in him, rooted and built up in him and established in the faith, just as you were taught, abounding in thanksgiving" (2:6–7).

They walked as they welcomed. The most important word in these verses is the two-letter word *so*. As you welcomed Jesus, *so* walk in Jesus. The way we go on with Christ must mirror the way we came to Christ.

The second most important word is *walk*. This is the word for a lifestyle, a consistent and continuous pattern of living.

The third most important word is *in*. We might have expected *with*. Walk *with* Christ. But instead Paul told them to walk *in* Christ. They were to live in the area of Christ, in the sphere of Christ, in the atmosphere of Christ, in the environment of Christ. Christ was to be the air they breathed. Paul defined this further in four ways.

- *Christ is our soil.* We walk in Jesus by being *rooted* in Jesus. Put deeper and wider roots into Jesus for a stronger and higher tree.
- *Christ is our foundation.* We walk in Jesus by being *built up* in Jesus. We don't ever move away from this foundation if we want to be built up spiritually.

- *Christ is our seal.* We walk in Jesus by being *established* in the faith. *Established* means "confirmed" and describes a court process of sealing a legal document so it can never be changed.
- *Christ is our wine.* We walk in Jesus by *abounding in thanksgiving.* The word *abounding* is used for an overflowing cup. Our degree of thankfulness reveals our Christology (which means what we know about Christ's person and work).

Christology is not an optional extra
but a source of safety and maturity.

Changing Our Story with God's Story

Sometimes we can complicate spiritual growth. We look around for the latest spiritual fad, trend, technique, or key. But Paul points us back to the beginning: As you began, so continue. You began by welcoming Christ as Jesus and Lord, then started walking in Christ as your soil, foundation, seal, and wine. Keep welcoming and walking like that to progress and grow.

Summary: How do I go forward in the Christian life? *As you began by welcoming Christ and walking in Christ, so continue to welcome him and walk in him.*

Question: What can you learn from how you began the Christian life to help you grow in the Christian life?

Prayer: Savior, I welcome you as Jesus, as Christ, and as Lord. I walk in you as my soil, foundation, seal, and wine.

Christless Christianity is the devil's Christianity.

34

Christless Christianity

COLOSSIANS 2:8-10

Fill in the blank: I'm not _____ enough. What word did you insert? I'm not good enough? Clever enough? Tall enough? Thin enough? Popular enough? Rich enough? Happy enough? When our identity is defined by what we're not, it's no surprise if we feel empty. *How do we find a full and fulfilling identity?*

The theme of Colossians is *Christ is enough, therefore I am enough.* That's why the devil is so focused on cultivating Christless Christianity and why Paul was so focused on cultivating Christ-full Christianity in Colossians 2:8–10. He starts by warning about the dangers of Christless Christianity.

Christless Christianity Is Empty and Deadly 2:8

Paul warns against Christless Christianity in four ways.

Christless Christianity is a snare. "See to it that no one takes you captive" (2:8). Paul is warning about spiritual predators, soul-traffickers who want to snatch us and carry us off. If Christ is not in first and central place, we've been kidnapped and are in extreme danger.

Christless Christianity is empty. It captures souls "by philosophy and empty deceit" (2:8). The Gnostics (Know-It-Alls) claimed to be philosophers (lovers of knowledge) who had "fullness" of knowledge. No, Paul says, you're utterly empty. You don't have Christ in first and central place, so you have nothing. This is a fraud not fullness.

Christless Christianity is humanistic. This philosophy is "according to human tradition" (2:8). It did not come from above, as the elitists claimed, but from below; not from God but from mere human minds.

Christless Christianity is demonic. Christless Christianity is "according to the elemental spirits of the world, and not according to Christ" (2:8). Ultimately it was constructed not just in human minds but in the devil's mind.

*Christless Christianity is
the devil's Christianity.*

*"If Christless Christianity is so dangerous,
how can I stay safe?"
Christ-full Christianity.*

Christ Is Full and Fulfilling 2:9–10

Paul urges a Christ-full Christianity.

Christ is full of God. "For in him the whole fullness of deity dwells bodily" (2:9). If you want to talk about fullness, here's real fullness. Christ is fully God and fully man. Imagine going to Lake Michigan with a little jar and trying to fill the jar with the entire lake. That's impossible, you say. But God filled the jar of a human body with his whole Godhead. With us this is impossible, but with God all things are possible.

Christ fills his people. "And you have been filled in him" (2:10). Here's Paul's logic: God is fully in Christ. You are fully in Christ. Therefore you are full in Christ. The Colossians were hearing from the Gnostics that Christ is not enough. You need more. Paul answers, "If you have Christ, you have all you need. If you have Christ, you have the fullness of God, and you cannot lose it."

Christ is full of power. "[He] is the head of all rule and authority" (2:10). Paul says to the Gnostics, "Don't talk to me about your principalities and powers. Let me talk to you about the head of all principalities and powers."

When you tell yourself, "I'm not enough," reply,
"In Christ I'm more than enough."

Changing Our Story with God's Story

None of us feel full because none of us are full and none of us can fill ourselves. We certainly try on different identities thinking they will feel good and look good, but they leave us empty. I'm fifty-five, and I still have to fight off man-made and devil-made identities as much as any teen. I still need to remind myself, "The full Christ fills me fully, and therefore I am fulfilled."

Summary: How do we find a full and fulfilling identity? *Ask God to fill you with the fullness of Christ and find your full and fulfilling identity in him.*

Question: How will you develop a more Christ-full identity?

Prayer: Filler, you have filled Christ with all fullness, therefore fill me with Christ that I may be full.

Our eyes see one
death on the cross;
our faith sees
multiple deaths
on the cross.

35

You Died Two Thousand Years Ago

COLOSSIANS 2:11-12

What possible connection can the dusty streets of Jerusalem in AD 30 have with our high-tech lives in AD 2021? In the age of TikTok, how does a naked, bloodied, and bruised body hanging on a wooden cross outside Jerusalem have any connection with my life? There seems to be a chasm—a geographical, chronological, and cultural chasm—between Christ's death and our lives. *How can we close the distance and connect with Christ's cross?* The apostle Paul builds a bridge for us in Colossians 2:11-12.

We Died in Christ 2:11

"In him also you were circumcised with a circumcision made without hands, by putting off the body of the flesh, by the circumcision of Christ" (2:11).

Christ was circumcised. Circumcision involved cutting off a small piece of flesh and throwing it away to die. Although designed by God to initiate entry into covenant relationship with him, here it's used as a picture of Christ's death. Not just a small piece of flesh, but his whole body was violently cut off and thrown aside to die.

We were circumcised with Christ. "In him you also were circumcised." Believers were in Christ when he was circumcised (cut off to die) on Calvary. He represented them so perfectly that they are regarded as having been as present as he was and as circumcised (cut off to die) as he was.

Ours was a "circumcision made without hands." Although Christ was physically cut off and cast aside, faith in Christ unites us with him so perfectly that we are regarded as circumcised, without suffering the same as he did by human hands.

"By putting off the body of the flesh." When we are united to Christ by faith, we are to regard our bodies of sinful flesh as put off to die. Just as Christ's sin-bearing body was cut off at Calvary, so the body of our sins is to be viewed as put off at Calvary. It's not only Christ who was put to death on the cross; every believer and all our sins were killed there too.

Our eyes see one death on the cross;
our faith sees multiple deaths on the cross.

If I died in Christ, does that mean
I was buried with him too?

We Were Buried in Christ 2:12

". . . having been buried with him in baptism" (2:12).

To *baptize* can mean to engulf, to overwhelm, or to dip. Here it refers to Christ's overwhelming and engulfing experience of death, especially his burial. Believers participated not only in Christ's death but also in his burial. We were so integrated with him that God sees us as having been entombed with him.

Our eyes see Christ in a lifeless grave,
but our faith sees Christ in a life-giving grave.

If I died and was buried with Christ,
was I resurrected with him too?

We Were Raised with Christ 2:12

"In which you were also raised with him through faith in the powerful working of God, who raised him from the dead" (2:12).

We were crucified on Easter Friday, buried on Easter Saturday, and in the garden on Easter Sunday. There is no closer union than that of the believer with Christ in his death, burial, and resurrection. Just as Christ left death behind and started a whole new powerful life, so faith in Christ accomplishes the same thing for the believer.

Our eyes see one empty tomb,
but our faith sees our empty tomb.

Changing Our Story with God's Story

No matter when or where we live, Paul's bridge will connect us with Christ and Christ with us. As soon as we take the first step on this bridge by faith, we are transported all the way to Calvary.

Summary: How can we close the distance and connect with Christ's cross? *Believe you died, were buried, and were raised with Christ, and then Christ's cross will be close and personal.*

Question: How does this triple union with Christ change your identity?

Prayer: Uniter, give me a new view of myself united to Christ so that I see myself dead, buried, and resurrected in him.

Christ was stripped of his clothes, but he stripped the devil of power.

36

Spiritual Resurrection

COLOSSIANS 2:13-15

Forgetfulness can be fatal. Sometimes, our forgetfulness has limited consequences (e.g., forgetting to wash our car). Other times, our forgetfulness has far greater consequences (e.g., forgetting to put gas in the car). But there's a forgetfulness that has even more serious consequences. As Christians, we sometimes forget how spiritually dead we were before Christ gave us life.

Why is this so serious? When we forget how spiritually dead we were, we forget how desperate our condition was (which undermines humility), we forget how bad our future was (which undermines gratitude), and we forget how great God's life-giving power was (which undermines worship).

How do we cure spiritual amnesia? In Colossians 2:13-15, Paul reminds the Colossians and us that we need spiritual resurrection as much as Christ's resurrection.

Spiritual Resurrection Is Necessary 2:13

"And you, who were dead in your trespasses and the uncircumcision of your flesh" (2:13). The Colossians were as spiritually responsive to God as a dead body is to human voices. That's zero response. Not a spark of spiritual life, vitality, energy, or grace. They were physically alive but spiritually dead, due to the sins they had committed and their separation from God's covenant family.

Remember you were dead, and then you will love life.

Our condition is desperate and our need is great.
Is there any hope?

Spiritual Resurrection Is an Act of God 2:13

". . . God made [you] alive together with him . . ." (2:13). The Colossians, who were dead as dead could be, are now more alive than they had ever been. What changed? God made them alive. The same power that raised Christ from the dead in verse 12 raised them from the dead when they were converted. God breathed life into their entombed souls, and they lived. God unilaterally did this by bringing them into contact with Jesus Christ. "God made you alive together with him." When we come into contact with Jesus by faith, we are resurrected.

To live apart from God is death;
to live together with Christ is life.

That's an astonishing possibility, but how can God do this?
We deserve death, so how can he give us life?

Spiritual Resurrection Is Secured by Forgiveness 2:13–15

". . . having forgiven us all our trespasses, by canceling the record of debt that stood against us with its legal demands" (2:13–14). God made the Colossians alive by forgiving their sins through Christ's cross-work. Christ has taken our long list of crimes and wiped it out. They are cancelled, obliterated, and expunged. "This he set aside, nailing it to the cross" (2:14). Every Christian's every sin was nailed to that tree and blotted out with Christ's blood. Forgiveness cancels our legal debt.

"He disarmed the rulers and authorities and put them to open shame, by triumphing over them in him" (2:15). The demons of hell were armed to the teeth when they attacked Christ with all their fury. But Christ won and they lost. They are now disarmed, defeated, despoiled, disabled, discredited, and dethroned. He is victorious, triumphant, jubilant, acclaimed, and glorified.

Christ was stripped of his clothes,
but he stripped the devil of power.

Changing Our Story with God's Story

I've found that the more I remember how dead I was in the past, the more spiritual life and liveliness I have now. I especially notice a deepening of humility, a widening of gratitude, and a lengthening of worship. Although I do not enjoy remembering who and what I was before Christ saved me, I know it is good for me and glorifying to Jesus.

Summary: How do we cure spiritual amnesia? *Remember how necessary, unilateral, and secure our spiritual resurrection is to maximize humility, gratitude, and worship.*

Question: How can you remind yourself of your resurrected identity so that you never forget it?

Prayer: Resurrector, remind me constantly of how dead I was so that I can praise you for how alive I am.

Come out of the shadows and into the Son.

 Hear God's Story | Change Your Story | Tell the Story | Change Others' Stories

37

Freedom from Lawyers, Mystics, and Monks

COLOSSIANS 2:16–23

Fullness and freedom! Two great longings of the human spirit. We want to be full and we want to be free. We want to be full of goodness and free from evil. We want to be satisfied and we want to be safe.

That's what Christianity offers the human spirit: fullness in Christ and freedom in Christ. That's why the devil attacks the Christian's fullness and freedom. That's what he was attacking in Colossae and what he's still attacking today. *How do we get and keep fullness and freedom in Christ?* In Colossians 2:16–23, Paul warns of three threats. And he trains us—not in self-defense but in Christ-defense.

Christ Frees Us from Condemning Lawyers 2:16–17

The apostle was watching religious lawyers impose unnecessary religious rules and regulations on every area of the Colossians' lives and said, "Let no one pass judgment on you in questions of food and drink, or with regard to a festival or a new moon or a Sabbath. These are a shadow of the things to come, but the substance belongs to Christ" (2:16–17).

The ceremonial rules of the Old Testament were mere shadows. They had a purpose in preparing for Christ and pointing to Christ, but the substance, the body of Christ, has now come, and therefore believers don't need the shadows anymore.

Come out of the shadows and into the Son.

We got rid of the lawyers!
But who's that white-robed person?

Christ Frees Us from Superior Mystics 2:18–19

Mystics rob us of our reward, Paul warned—not our heavenly reward but our earthly joy in Christ (2:18–19). The mystics claimed to be enriching the Colossians, but they were stealing from them. How? While holding tenaciously to their allegedly superior worship, visions, and spirituality, in the process they lost their hold on Christ (2:19). If we lose contact with our head (Christ), we lose our source of life, nourishment, and growth.

Although the mystics said they had superior-tasting spiritual food, Paul said that it was junk food. It was high in carbs and sugar, but it lacked protein. Don't substitute sugar for steak.

Mystics promise higher life
but make us feel like lower life.

We got rid of the mystics.
But who's the guy in the black robe?

Christ Frees Us from Worldly Monks 2:20–23

Secular worldliness can be seen in parties, drugs, materialism, and so on. But Paul introduces us to another kind of worldliness: *religious worldliness.* He calls it "the elemental [or basic] spirits of the world" (2:20). Although this worldliness has a religious face, it is grounded in the same basic worldly principles found in all ungodly lifestyles. Paul cautions that this unbiblical religion is oppressive ("you submit to regulations"), humanistic ("according to human precepts and teachings"), deceptive ("these have indeed an appearance of wisdom"), and powerless ("they are of no value in stopping the indulgence of the flesh").

Paul therefore unleashes his most potent weapon to take down the monk-monster. It's a cross-shaped sword with a double edge: (1) you died with Christ, and (2) you died to worldliness. Christ's death released us from the secular world's pleasures and the religious world's powers. We are now free to live with a new identity in an entirely new world, the world of Christ's law and order.

Monks wear dark robes
but can't change dark hearts.

Changing Our Story with God's Story

We all have weak spots. For me, it's the lawyers that usually empty me and enslave me. For you it may be the mystics or the monks. But whatever our weak spot, we have a strong Savior to fill us and free us again and again.

Summary: How do we get and keep fullness and freedom in Christ? *Use the fullness of Christ to free you from identity-stealing lawyers, mystics, and monks.*

Question: Which is the biggest threat to your spiritual fullness and freedom: lawyers, mystics, or monks?

Prayer: Filler and Free-er, fill me and free me with my identity in Christ so that I can be satisfied and safe.

A change of worldview will change our self-view.

38

Living in Heaven on Earth

COLOSSIANS 3:1-4

Has anyone ever told you, "You need to change?" and you've wondered what on earth she was talking about? She could see it but you couldn't.

Or perhaps you did see it, but replied, "I know, but I don't want to change." Or, "I know, I want to change, and I've tried to change, but I just can't." Or, "I'm trying, but the change is so slow and small." Personal change is hard.

How does personal change happen? In Colossians 3:1-4, Paul takes us to heaven to find a new identity that can change our lives on earth.

Heaven Changes Our View of Change 3:1-2

The first obstacle to overcome in personal change is how we see ourselves. Although others can see we need to change, often we can't see it ourselves. That's why the apostle begins by giving us a different perspective on ourselves. He helps us see ourselves differently.

"You have been raised with Christ . . . seated at the right hand of God" (3:1). United to Christ by faith, we are there with him as he reigns over the universe. That changes our view of the world and of ourselves, doesn't it?

A change of worldview will change our self-view.

But how do I increase my desire for change?

Heaven Changes Our Desire for Change 3:1–2

"If then you have been raised with Christ, seek the things that are above" (3:1). When Christians on earth see their position and identity in heaven, they will begin to seek heavenly things on earth. Paul is not urging detachment from and disinterest in this earth. It's more about what we look at first and most. If we first look above, and then look at things below, we will feel the contrast between heaven and earth and the desire for change will become irresistible.

Changing our desires changes our desire for change.

But what about the power to change?

Heaven Changes Our Power to Change 3:3–4

Where is the power of the Christian life? Christians rely on many alternative energy sources: personality, willpower, drive, inspiration, confidence, and so on. But none of these gives power for deep and long-term change. For that we must look outside of ourselves to Christ.

You died with Christ (3:3). Just as death is the separation of the body from the soul, so this death is a separation of the old life from the new life and releases Christ's new life into ours. "For you have died, and your life is hidden with Christ in God" (3:3). *Hidden* means that we have a secret and private power source that others cannot see, and sometimes even we cannot see.

When you have no power to change, change your power to change.

But will I have changed enough by judgment day?

Heaven Changes Our Hope of Change 3:4

When discouraged by how little you've changed, remind yourself of the future heavenly change that lies ahead. Christ will appear in glory, and you will appear with Christ in glory (3:4). Christ's hidden glory will be revealed, and so will yours.

Change is hopeless without hope of change.

Changing Our Story with God's Story

If you were to ask me in what area I most desired change, I would say prayer. I've been a Christian for more than thirty years, and I've seen God change me for good in a number of ways. But when it comes to prayer, I fear I'm still a baby Christian. I'm hoping that this text's description of my being raised with Christ to God's right hand will be the catalyst for prayer. If I can remember that I am already raised with Christ and seated with him on his throne at the right hand of God, I will change—and so will my prayers.

Summary: How does personal change happen? *Live in heaven on earth for heavenly change on earth.*

Question: How can you change your self-view to change yourself?

Prayer: Change-Maker, change me by giving me desires to change, power to change, and hope of change.

Put on the New You label if you want a New You lifestyle.

39

Designer-Label Christianity

COLOSSIANS 3:5-11

Our labels determine our lifestyle. Recently I've been working hard at improving my diet and fitness. One of the greatest helps has been Under Armour clothes! I'm not being paid to say this, but since I started wearing more Under Armour T-shirts and shorts, I've found it easier to adopt an Under Armour lifestyle. My kids now mockingly call me Mr. Under Armour. The label has become part of my identity which in turn changes my lifestyle. The label changes the way I view myself and the way I live. Our labels determine our lifestyle.

Spiritually, there are only two designer brands: Old You and New You. Like all designer labels, these spiritual brands also define our identity and determine our lifestyle. They decide who we are and what we do. So, *how can we use our label to change our lifestyle?* In Colossians 3:5-8, we're told the first step is to rip off our Old You label.

The "Old You" Label Is Dead 3:5-9

"Put to death therefore what is earthly in you" (3:5). You died to sin with Christ in the past . . . therefore kill sin in the present. "Put to death" is strong language. It means murder sin, execute it, slay it, get rid of it, bury it, and turn it to dust. This is a fight to the death. This is not a sparring match, this is not shadowboxing, this isn't even UFC (Ultimate Fighting Championship). A knockout is not enough. You have to kill, or you will be killed.

Paul is commissioning special forces to target special sins, starting with sexual sin and money sin (3:5–7). When it comes to verbal sins, he changes the image from murdering to putting off, or unclothing (3:8–9).

The Message captures the idea well: "You're done with that old life. It's like a filthy set of ill-fitting clothes you've stripped off and put in the fire" (Col. 3:9). Say of these old clothes, "I wouldn't be seen dead in these."

Put off the Old You label,
or you'll live the Old You sins.

"Is it all negative? Put this to death, put this off.
Anything positive?" Yes, there is hope of new you too!

The "New You" Label Is Alive 3:10–11

"[You] have put on the new self, which is being renewed in knowledge after the image of its creator" (3:10).

You rose again with new life in Christ, therefore live a new life for Christ. You have new life, therefore wear new clothes. Holiness is halved if we are only putting off. We must also put on.

The new you has a new image. You are "renewed . . . after the image of its creator" (3:10). You have a new stylist, a new wardrobe consultant, the designer who wants to see his image, his brand upon you.

The new you is "renewed in knowledge" (3:10). The New You label isn't just a different look; it's a different way of thinking about everything and everybody. "Here there is not Greek and Jew, circumcised and uncircumcised, barbarian, Scythian, slave, free; but Christ is all, and in all" (3:11). The New You label replaces barriers with bridges and divisions with unity. Christ is all that matters and is in all that matters.

Put on the New You label if
you want a New You lifestyle.

Changing Our Story with God's Story

As we notice the difference different clothes make to our identity, thinking, and lifestyle, let's remember how different spiritual clothes change our identity, thinking, and lifestyle. I want Christ's armor to make a much bigger difference to me than Under Armour.

Summary: How do we use our label to change our lifestyle? *Put off the Old You label and live up to the New You label to change who you are and what you do.*

Question: What rags is God calling you to put off today, and what robes is he asking you to wear today?

Prayer: Designer, thank you for helping me to see how horrible my old wardrobe was and for giving me a whole new wardrobe of designer wear.

We don't need a new worship style so much as a new worship heart.

Hear
God's Story

Change
Your Story

Tell
the Story

Change
Others' Stories

40

Holistic Christianity

COLOSSIANS 3:12-17

Many in our society want change. But when you ask, *What needs to be changed most and how do we make change last?* people can't agree on either question.

In Colossians 3:12–17, Paul tells us what must change first and how to effect lasting change. He is addressing two temptations that faced the Colossians and have faced all Christians through the ages.

- Some Christians limit personal renewal to their internal and invisible world.
- Some Christians focus on outward change but the change has no inward foundation or power.

Paul, therefore, shows the Colossians how to pursue renewal in every area of life.

Relational Renewal Starts Inside but Doesn't Stop There 3:12-15

God wants to see change in the Colossians' lives, and he starts with inner change not outer change. That's why Paul begins with a new inner identity: "Put on then, as God's chosen ones, holy and beloved" (3:12). Colossians, you are God's chosen ones, holy ones, and loved ones. But that identity change on the inside results in an outer change in lifestyle.

That new lifestyle involves new compassion, kindness, humility, gentleness, and patience (3:12). It calls believers to forgive others because Christ has forgiven them, moving again from inside to out-side (3:13). Three other inner-to-outer changes are new love, new peace, and new gratitude (3:14–16).

All these changes start in the heart, our invisible inner life, our relationship with God. But they result in evident changes in our visible outer life, in our relationships with others.

Renew your relationship with God
to renew your relationships with others.

"How can we thank God for such renewal of our relationships?"
By singing to God and to one another.

Song Renewal Starts Inside but Doesn't Stop There 3:16

Again, Paul starts with inner renewal. "Let the word of Christ dwell in you richly" (3:16). *Dwell* here means to soak or marinate. Christ's word will give you a distinctive inner flavor that will seep out in audible songs.

Inner renewal of receiving Christ's word results in outer renewal of singing Christ's word. We sing to one another, "teaching and admonishing one another in all wisdom, singing psalms and hymns and spiritual songs (3:16). And we sing to God "with thankfulness in your hearts to God" (3:16).

We don't need a new worship style
so much as a new worship heart.

Are there any areas where
outer change comes first?

All Renewal Starts Inside but Doesn't Stop There 3:17

Outside renewal must start with but not stop with inside renewal. But just in case anyone thinks that there's any part of life this doesn't apply to, Paul says: "And whatever you do, in word or deed, do everything in the name of the Lord Jesus, giving thanks to God the Father through him" (3:17).

"Do everything in the name of the Lord Jesus" reflects inner renewal. We are to do everything out of love for Christ, for Christ's glory, like Christ would, and depending upon Christ. "Giving thanks to God the Father through him" demonstrates outside renewal.

Christianity is all or nothing. It's an all-encompassing religion. It changes the entire inside life to change the entire outside life.

*We'll never change anything outside
unless we change everything inside.*

Changing Our Story with God's Story

The biggest changes have occurred in my life as a result of concentrating on my new identity in Christ. Nothing changes my desires and delights so much as remembering who I am in Christ. When I get that *who* right, *what's* right always follows. Inside change produces outside change.

Summary: What most needs to be changed, and how do we make change last? *On the basis of inside renewal, pursue outside renewal in every area of life for powerful change and witness.*

Question: What most needs to be changed in your life, and how does this passage guide your plan for change?

Prayer: Renewer, I bring my whole self to you for inner change that will produce outside change.

When each gives
up self, each gains
more for self.

 Hear | Change | Tell | Change
God's Story | Your Story | the Story | Others' Stories

41

The Simple Secret to a Happy Marriage

COLOSSIANS 3:18–19

Marriage is in a mess, and therefore we are in a mess. Marriage is being redefined (man-man, woman-woman, polygamy, polyamory), and way too many marriages end in divorce.

It's not just marriage in general that's in trouble; our own marriage may be in trouble. Yet there are some marriages that are truly happy. *What's the secret to a happy marriage?* God shares his answer in Colossians 3:18–19.

A Happy Marriage Is Defined by God 3:18–19

Verses 18–19 assume four basic points. (1) A husband is a man; (2) A wife is a woman; (3) A man can only marry a woman (and vice versa); (4) A man can only marry one woman (and vice versa).

This isn't conservative Christianity. This is biblical Christianity. We cannot set the Bible aside and think things will get better. Exhibit A: our society and culture. Although the media tell us we are being unloving in limiting love, the rates of unhappiness are far higher for those who abandon God's definition of marriage.[4]

If we don't limit love, we limit happiness.

---

4 Lyman Stone, "Does Getting Married Really Make You Happier?," *Institute for Family Studies*, https://ifstudies.org/.

So why is marriage so messed up?

A Happy Marriage Has One Main Challenge 3:18–19

The challenge is selfishness, also known as self-centeredness, self-focus, or self-serving. These are different expressions for the same thing: *me-first*.

The wrong question to ask, therefore, is, How can my wife make me happy? Or, How can my husband make me happy? Those questions are a recipe for disaster.

Selfishness is self-destruction.

So what's the right question?

A Happy Marriage Has One Essential Ingredient 3:18–19

The right question is, How do I change to make my spouse happy? That's selflessness, and it involves giving up by both men and women, though in different ways.

The wife gives up self-will. Paul commands: "Wives, submit to your husbands, as is fitting in the Lord" (3:18). *Submission* conjures up pictures of slavery, abuse, servility, and inferiority. But biblical submission starts with equality. Men and women are essentially equal in dignity, value, gifts, intellect, and spirituality.

Also, biblical submission is voluntary not coerced. While maintaining her essential equality, a wife selflessly chooses to give up her functional equality, for the sake of better functioning of the marriage. That doesn't mean there's no discussion or debate between spouses. It means that if disagreement persists, a wife submits her will to her husband's.

"As is fitting in the Lord" can also mean "As matches what Jesus did." He maintained essential equality while submitting to his Father's authority for the sake of his people (John 4:34; 5:30; 6:38).

So if the wife gives up her self-will, what does the husband give up? He gives up his self-love. "Husbands, love your wives, and do not be harsh with them" (3:19).

Love is the giving of one's entire self for the good of another. That brings us to another *s* word that's not very popular today: *sacrifice*. This is not a "falling in love" kind of love but a Calvary kind of love. It's giving up one's well-being for the well-being of another. The most important question in marriage is not, What can I get out of it? but, What can I give to it/her? Both spouses have to give up first place. Both give up in different ways. The wife gives up self-will; the husband gives up self-love.

When each gives up self,
each gains more for self.

Changing Our Story with God's Story

Almost nothing else in the Bible is harder to believe than this. There's also nothing more countercultural than self-denial. But it's God's simple secret to a happy marriage and a happy culture.

Summary: What is the simple secret to a happy marriage? *Be selfless for a gospel-shaped happy marriage.*

Question: How will you give up self for the good of another?

Prayer: Self-Giver, give me self-giving so that I give good to others and glory to you, and therefore I gain in the long run.

Change your world: obey your parents.

42

Pleasing God by Pleasing Parents

COLOSSIANS 3:20

I know a number of families that use this book for their daily devotions. So here I want to speak to you kids. I'll chat with the parents next.

Most of you finished school with a report card from your teachers on how well (or badly) you did in various subjects, didn't you? Well, God has a report card for every child, but it has just one subject on it: Obedience to Parents. It has a verse written at the top: "Children, obey your parents in everything, for this pleases the Lord" (Col. 3:20).

How many families would be transformed if this short verse were practiced? So let's ask, *How does a complete Christ completely change children?*

Obey Your Parents to Please Your Parents 3:20

"Children, obey your parents in everything" (3:20). *Obedience* is not a fashionable or popular word, but whatever else a child is to be, he or she is to be obedient. That simply means doing what you are told by your dad or mom. What does this obedience look like in day-to-day life?

Total obedience: "Obey . . . in everything." Do everything your parents say unless it's clearly contrary to God's word (Eph. 6:1).

Cheerful obedience: Obey not with an angry and moody face but willingly and happily. God is not asking you to obey a dictator but parents who love you, care for you, and provide for you.

Secret obedience: This means obeying even when your parents are not there to see. That's when we really know if our obedience is real or just pretend.

Change your world:
obey your parents.

My obedience pleases my parents,
but what do I get out of it?

Obey Your Parents to Please God 3:20

"Children, obey your parents in everything, . . . for this pleases the Lord" (3:20)

The Bible contains many encouragements to obey parents. This verse supplies the greatest motivation of all: you will please God. When God sees obedience to our parents, it delights him. When he sees disobedience, it disgusts him.

Why is obeying our parents so important to God? Your parents are God's representatives in your life. He has appointed them to rule you in his name. The way you talk and listen to them reveals how you talk and listen to God. The state of your relationship with them reveals the state of your relationship with God. You cannot please God if you are not pleasing your parents. You can please God by pleasing your parents. That's a powerful motive to obedience, isn't it?

When I was a kid, I used to dream that maybe one day the teachers would get mixed up and mistakenly send me home with the class genius's report card. With Christ's coming, that dream has come true and is even better than I could have imagined.

Jesus lived the perfect childhood, the perfect life, that we cannot. He then put our name on the top of the report card and wrote, "This is your new identity. Take it to Father." Christ's report card can become ours by faith. He hands us his perfect report and says,

"Write your name on the top." What a happy day! What a happy eternity!

Change your relationship with God
by changing your relationship with your parents.

Changing Our Story with God's Story

When I look back on my childhood, I can see many times when I messed up by disobeying my parents. I'd love to go back and put things right, but I can't. However, Christ took my imperfect report card and nailed it to the cross. Then he gave me his perfect report card instead. God was pleased, my parents were pleased, and I was pleased.

Summary: How does a complete Christ completely change children? *Obey your parents in everything to please God, and look to the perfect Son when you fail.*

Question: How can you increase your obedience to your parents and therefore the pleasure you give to God?

Prayer: Father, thank you for being the perfect parent and giving me a perfect identity in your Son. Help me to obey my imperfect parents to give you perfect pleasure.

Change your relationship with God by changing your relationship with your children.

Hear
God's Story

Change
Your Story

Tell
the Story

Change
Others' Stories

43

Daddy Deprivation

COLOSSIANS 3:21

One of the biggest crises our culture is facing is the failure of fatherhood, the failure of men to become what God has created them to be, that is, models of God's fatherhood to their children. Blake Wilson calls this crisis, "Daddy Deprivation," a crisis that pastor and author Eric Mason says, "crosses cultural and socio-economic grounds; it's a crisis prevalent in all areas of society, for the *absence of a father leaves a lasting void in a man's identity and development.*"[5]

For many, this vacuum is being filled with the phenomenon of "internet dads," men on YouTube or social media who instruct young people on "dad things." The Bible, though, forbids the outsourcing of fatherhood, but rather calls dads to step up and do their duty. "Fathers, do not provoke your children, lest they become discouraged" (3:21). *How do we discourage our children?* The most common problem is in how we discipline them.

Discipline Is Painful 3:21

Although we're about to flag many parenting pitfalls in disciplining our children, the difficulty does not excuse the duty. This verse warns against errors in discipline, but that still implies the exhortation to discipline our children as the Lord would discipline them (Eph. 6:4).

This requires setting boundaries in connection with digital technology, media use, friends, home-time, bedtime, vocabulary, and so on. But it also involves painful consequences when the limits are crossed—pain for them, which might cause even greater pain for us.

---

5   Eric Mason, *Manhood Restored* (Nashville: B&H, 2013), 3.

It often takes a lot of courageous faith to believe this pain is worth it, but it's a duty that God blesses to them and us, as we both learn about God's fatherly heart in different ways.

***Change your relationship with God by
changing your relationship with your children.***

So where do we usually go wrong in this duty?

Discipline Can Be Provocative 3:21

Colossians 3:21 cautions against discipline that exasperates and embitters our children into angry rebellion against us, making the situation and them worse rather than better. Sadly, there are many ways to do this, including:

- *Excessive discipline*: too often (for every infraction) or too hard.
- *Disproportionate discipline*: way out of scale to the offense.
- *Inconsistent discipline*: the child punished for one offense one day but not on other days.
- *Prejudiced discipline*: unfairly favoring one child over another.
- *Unexplained discipline*: no explanation of the *why*, therefore no understanding by the child.
- *Unforgiving discipline*: despite the child saying *sorry*, the father keeps the child under a cloud for days/weeks after the discipline.
- *Imbalanced discipline*: discipline not balanced with encouragement or praise for things done right.
- *Humiliating discipline*: aims to belittle and shame.
- *Public discipline*: no attempt to hide the child's offenses and punishment from others.
- *Bad-tempered discipline*: terrifyingly out of control.
- *Prayerless discipline*: no prayer before, during, or after the discipline.
- *Heartless discipline*: no attempt to get behind the *why* of the wrong and show the child the need for heart-change.

- *Unwarned discipline*: the child was not previously instructed about what was wrong or warned about the wrong before the discipline.
- *Selfish discipline*: Dad takes out his own frustrations on the child to make himself feel better.
- *Gospel-less discipline*: no hope of divine or parental forgiveness. Christ's atoning sacrifice is ignored.

When we provoke our kids to anger, we provoke God to anger, resulting in God disciplining us for our sinful discipline of our children.

God disciplines us perfectly for our imperfect discipline.

Changing Our Story with God's Story

Dads, let's confess our failures to God, our children, and our wives. Let's repent and believe the gospel all over again to cleanse and encourage us. Wives, encourage and challenge your husbands to take such roles and assume such responsibilities.

Summary: How do we discourage our children? *Discourage your children by avoiding discipline and by engaging in sinful discipline.*

Question: Fathers, will you confess your failure to discipline and failures in discipline to your children, your wife, and God?

Prayer: Perfect Father, I confess my imperfect discipline that has damaged and discouraged my children. Please forgive me and give me your fatherly Spirit so I can embrace and exhibit your fatherhood better.

If we're discipled by God, we can disciple for God.

 Hear God's Story | Change Your Story | Tell the Story | Change Others' Stories

44

Daddy Discipleship

COLOSSIANS 3:21

We don't become fathers when we become fathers. Or to put it another way, when we have children, we don't automatically become perfect fathers. When we hold our first child, we're just beginning lifelong learning about fatherhood. There is no more important subject to learn if we are to be encouragers of our children.

In the last chapter, we learned about disciplining our children; now we will look at *discipling* our children. Although Colossians 3:21 is a warning, every warning in the Bible implies a positive duty. On the flip side of this warning against bad discipline is an exhortation to good discipling, and good discipling of our children begins with God's discipling of us as fathers. *What does dad discipleship look like?*

Dad Disciples Begin with Unlearning 3:21

We have to begin with unlearning—unlearning some of the unbiblical models of fatherhood we may have absorbed growing up. There are three models or stereotypes of fatherhood that we must bring to Scripture for deleting or editing:

- *Cultural fatherhood:* We may have absorbed a Dutch, American, Scottish, or other national view of fatherhood.
- *Dad's fatherhood:* We may simply be copying our Dad's fatherhood.

- *Media fatherhood:* We may have adopted the kind of fatherhood most often portrayed in movies, ranging from macho extremes to effeminate extremes.

A faithful and fruitful relationship with our children begins by confessing and forsaking all unbiblical stereotypes, and by asking God to shape us with the Bible-type, God's fatherhood.

Cultural fatherhood will discourage our children;
scriptural fatherhood will encourage them.

What happens after unlearning the bad?

Dad Disciples Keep on Learning 3:21

Dad discipleship begins with a study plan. We study for school, careers, sport, and hobbies, but do we study fatherhood? If we are to avoid the negatives in Colossians 1:21 and fulfill the positives, we need a study plan. At the bare minimum this would include:

- Listen to a few sermons a year on fathering.
- Read a book a year on fathering.
- Ask an older dad about fathering.
- Pray about fathering and how to be a better dad.

How encouraging would it be for kids to see their dad studying how to be a better dad? Remember, the first area where God will assess our faith is not our careers but our families (Col. 3:18–25; Eph. 6:1–9).

Next, we need a model, because we learn not only by reading but by watching. There are three models of fatherhood in Scripture. The first is God's fatherly relationship with Israel (we have a whole Testament of training there). The second is Jesus Christ's fatherly relationship with his disciples. He said, "Whoever has seen me has seen the Father" (John 14:9). The third is God's adoption of us as his children, which also involves him sending his fatherly Spirit in our hearts (Rom. 8:15).

As we learn from God's model of fatherhood, we become models of God's fatherhood. Our children's view of us fathers is the greatest influence on their view of God as Father. What a solemn thought. We need God's help if we are to model him accurately to our children so that they want to become God's children.

If we're discipled by God, we can disciple for God.

Changing Our Story with God's Story

If you have (or have had) such an earthly father to disciple you, thank God that you have been blessed in this way. If you don't have, and maybe never have had, such an earthly father, you can get a perfect heavenly Father through faith in Christ (John 14:10). He is a good, good Father.

Summary: What does dad discipleship look like? *Unlearn unbiblical fatherhood, then study biblical models of fatherhood to encourage your children to thrive in every way.*

Question: What's your study plan to become a discipler of your children?

Prayer: Heavenly Father, disciple me so that I can be a better discipler of my children.

Work for God's joy, and you'll find joy in God and in your work.

Hear
God's Story

Change
Your Story

Tell
the Story

Change
Others' Stories

45

I Hate My Work

COLOSSIANS 3:22–4:1

"I hate my work. I hate my boss. I don't get paid enough." Don't worry, that's not me speaking. I'm quoting what I've heard many others say over the years. According to US job satisfaction statistics, 70 percent of all employees in the United States are not engaged or are actively disengaged with their work.[6]

Is getting another job the answer to employment dissatisfaction? For Christians, the first question shouldn't be, How do I get another job? but *How can I enjoy my job better?* Paul provides two joy multipliers for our jobs in Colossians 3:22–4:1.

Our Work Is for the Lord 3:22–23

In these verses Paul gives Christians the what, the why, and the how for our daily work.

First, what we do. We obey our bosses in everything. "Bondservants, obey in everything those who are your earthly masters" (3:22). He's speaking specifically to slaves in Colossae, but this is applicable to any of us with bosses. (Note that Paul is not *condoning* slavery but rather giving instructions to the slaves who were in Colossae.) *Everything* means "everything lawful." Our bosses have no right to add "sin" to our job description, and we have no right to obey if they do.

Second, why we work. We work to please God. "Not by way of eye-service, as people-pleasers . . . as for the Lord and not for men"

6   Jim Harter, "U.S. Employee Engagement Slump Continues," *Gallup*, April 25, 2022, https://www.gallup.com/.

(3:22–23). We are serving the Lord Jesus, therefore we keep our eyes on the Lord and remember we are working for him more than for any earthly boss. Behind our earthly boss is our heavenly boss, and therefore we work "with sincerity of heart, fearing the Lord" (3:22), knowing that he will punish us for duplicity. We want to please the Lord in our work.

Third, how we work. We work enthusiastically. "Whatever you do, work heartily, as for the Lord and not for men" (3:23). One of the reasons people are so disheartened at work is because they work half-heartedly. Work can fill our hearts if we work with all our hearts.

If we go into work every day with God's what, why, and how, we'll go home every day with God's blessing, smile, and pleasure.

Work for God's joy, and you'll
find joy in God and in your work.

But look at my paycheck.
Am I not worth more than that?

Our Work Is Rewarded by God 3:24–4:1

If we follow God's what, why, and how, he will reward us with a big bonus at the end of the day. ". . . knowing that from the Lord you will receive the inheritance as your reward" (3:24). That's a huge promise. We may get limited pay here, but we will get full pay in the hereafter. We may be paid less than others or less than we deserve or less than we can live on, but God will make it all up to us in heaven.

However, if we reject God's what, why, and how, we will get a big shock at the end of the day. "For the wrongdoer will be paid back for the wrong he has done, and there is no partiality" (3:25). It doesn't matter how much we earn or what promotions we gain or what titles we achieve, if we substitute our what, why, and how for God's, we will be paid back for the wrong we have done.

That's not just true for workers. It's also true for bosses. "Masters, treat your bondservants justly and fairly, knowing that you also have a Master in heaven" (4:1). Bosses will answer to *the* boss. Many millionaires will be eternally poor, while many faithful Christians will have more than they could ever imagine.

We may not be a millionaire on earth,
but we'll be a spiritual heir in heaven.

Changing Our Story with God's Story

Job dissatisfaction increased greatly during the COVID-19 pandemic, spawning the "The Great Resignation." When people are questioning their own employment, it can be an opportunity to change their stories about work with God's story about work.

Summary: How can I enjoy my job better? *Work to please God and get paid by God.*

Question: How will this new way of looking at yourself and your work change the way you work today?

Prayer: Everlasting Employer, make me a better employee and employer by working for your pleasure and pay.

Be a superglue pray-er not a glue stick pray-er.

46

Talk to God Better to Talk to Others Better

COLOSSIANS 4:2

I often feel guilty about how rarely and how badly I talk about my faith to others. I'm not talking about preaching—that's relatively easy—but about one-to-one witnessing. Sometimes I lack courage and fail to speak. Other times I lack care and fail to speak well.

Recently I asked myself, "How many times have I actually prayed for opportunities to speak to others about my faith? How many times have opportunities been given, and I didn't talk about my faith? How many times have I talked about my faith but messed up? How many times have I spoken, and spoken well, but then undermined that conversation by how I talk at other times?"

That made me ask, "How can I increase in courage and care when talking to others about God?" But Colossians 4:2 reminded me that talking to others about God begins with talking to God about others. So, the right question is, *How do I talk to God better so I can talk to others better?*

Talk to God Steadfastly 4:2

We are often tempted to give up praying for help in witnessing. But Paul says don't give up, "continue steadfastly in prayer" (4:2). Keep praying and praying and praying. The verb here means "adhere to" or "stick to." Stick with it with perseverance, determination, and resolve. We can continue steadfastly in prayer only by continuing steadfastly in the gospel.

So let's pray every day for opportunities to witness. Pray for opportunities with specific people. Even if we've missed or messed up opportunities in the past, let's stick with it.

Be a superglue pray-er
not a glue stick pray-er.

"What help does God give so I stick with it?"
He opens our eyes to see.

Talk to God Watchfully 4:2

"Being watchful in it" doesn't just mean watch that you don't give up. It also means to watch for opportunities, watch with expectancy for God to answer, watch for the answers, watch for more than you expected or asked for. This also implies open-eyed prayer not sleepy-eyed prayer. It's a call to energetic and lively prayer.

Though we may close our physical eyes when we pray, we're praying that God would keep our eyes open after prayer. We don't pray and forget, but pray and look out.

Be a dynamic pray-er not a drowsy pray-er.

What do I do when God answers prayer?

Talk to God Thankfully 4:2

"Being watchful in it with thanksgiving." If we're watchful, we will soon be thankful. We'll see God answer our prayers and rejoice with gratitude to him. Thanksgiving for past answers is massive motivation for future prayers.

Thanking God for giving us the gospel increases prayer for more gospel for others. Thanking God for those who spoke to us about

Jesus increases our speaking to others about Jesus. Thanking God for past fruitful opportunities to speak will increase prayer for more of the same.

If we lack stickability and energy in praying for the lost and if we are not praying for or taking opportunities, then the remedy is to increase gratitude to God.

Grateful pray-ers are great witnesses.

Changing Our Story with God's Story

Colossians 4:2 explains the witness of Jesus. Why was he so good at talking to others about God? It was because he was so good at talking to God about others. When we listen in on his prayers, we hear him "continue steadfastly in prayer, being watchful in it with thanksgiving" (4:2). His perfect prayers cover my imperfect prayers and even present them perfectly to God. What a motivation to be a more perfect witness!

Summary: How do I talk to God better so I can talk to others better? *Talk to God with patience, vigilance, and gratitude so that you can talk to others with success.*

Question: How will this change your daily prayers?

Prayer: Hearer of Prayer, teach me to talk to you better about others so I can talk to others better about you.

Prayer oils hinges and opens doors.

47

Gospel Clarity

COLOSSIANS 4:3–4

What is the gospel? If a five-year-old asked you this question, do you think you could answer it in a way that a five-year-old could understand? Or if someone who had never been to church before asked you the same question, could you explain the gospel simply enough for him to grasp? If we want to tell God's Story to others, we need to use words that are simple and clear enough for a child or a non-churchgoer to understand.

That's why Paul prays for gospel clarity in Colossians 4:3–4. He's just spoken to God (4:2) because he wants to speak to others about God (4:3–6). He talks to God constantly so that he can talk to others clearly. *What should we talk to God about when we want to talk to others about God?*

Ask for an Open Door for the Word 4:3

"That God may open to us a door for the word" (4:3). What closes the door? Two sets of rusty hinges. The first set of rusty hinges is on the other side of the door: people's lack of interest, lack of need, lack of time, lack of concern about sin. All of these close the door on one side. But the second set of rusty hinges is on our side: our coldness, our unbelief, our doubt, our selfishness. We therefore ask God to oil both sets of hinges.

Prayer oils hinges and opens doors.

What happens when the door opens?

Present the Living Person of the Word 4:3

Paul asks for an open door "to declare the mystery of Christ" (4:3). To declare a mystery is to make clear what was previously hidden, shadowy, or blurry. When God opens the door, we want to present Jesus as clearly as possible. We are to put Christ in front of people, not a system of doctrine, not a church, and not a pastor. We must not present just the benefits of the gospel but Christ who is the gospel. We speak not just about forgiveness or salvation but also Jesus the forgiver and Jesus the Savior.

The gospel is a person not a system.

So when I present Jesus,
will everyone believe?

Be Willing to Suffer for the Word 4:3

"On account of which I am in prison" (4:3). Paul is praying for an open door while staring at a locked door. He's locked up in prison because he walked through an open gospel door. He was willing to have the door slammed in his face for the sake of others seeing Christ's face. When God opens the door to witness, we must be ready to see a jail door close behind us.

When the door is slammed in your face,
remember it's so others may see Christ's face.

So should I perhaps hedge and dodge a bit?

Make a Clear Declaration of the Word 4:4

"That I may make it clear, which is how I ought to speak" (4:4). When tempted to muddy the waters a little, Paul asks for a filter to remove anything that would obscure his witness. "Lord, don't let me fudge or confuse or backpedal or soft-pedal. Remove mysticism and vague generalizations. Help me to be concrete and crystal clear. Help me speak so I will not be misunderstood."

Aim to be concrete and clear,
not to hedge and dodge.

Changing Our Story with God's Story

If we're not clear about the gospel ourselves, we won't be clear in telling others about it. That's why I find family devotions with my kids to be helpful. I'm forced to try to explain God's word in the simplest words possible. I find that harder than lecturing to PhD students. Family devotions help us practice this daily. If your kids are grown up and have left home, why not take some time to write down the gospel in the simplest terms you can manage? Imagine you were explaining it to someone who spoke with limited English. How would you commend Christ to him?

Summary: What should we talk to God about when we want to talk to others about God? *Pray for clarity and simplicity in presenting Jesus, even if we might suffer as a result.*

Question: What is the gospel? Can you explain the transformation of our identity in a hundred simple words?

Prayer: Clarifier, take away the fog of cowardice and confusion so that I may speak with courageous clarity about Jesus the identity restorer.

It's all very well to talk well, but we must also walk well.

48

Wise Walk + Wise Talk = Wise Witness

COLOSSIANS 4:5-6

What we say is important; how we say it is even more important. We might talk to others clearly but not talk to them carefully. We need a combination of clarity and care in talking to others. In the last chapter we worked on clarity; in this we want to work on care.

What happens if we don't take care in our witness? At best, our witness won't do any good. At worst, it will do a lot of harm. It's not just that we won't attract people to Jesus; we will make Jesus repulsive to them. Many are lost because we don't witness clearly; even more are lost because we don't witness carefully. Many are won with clarity; even more are won with care. A combination of clarity and care is a powerful magnet to Christ. *What does a careful witness look like?*

We Walk with Wisdom 4:5

A careful witness begins with a careful walk. "Walk in wisdom toward outsiders" (4:5). We are to be wise in how we live before others, especially before those outside the Christian faith. We will not get a hearing for Christ unless we are living like Christ. The first step in walking with wisdom is walking with him who is Wisdom. The more we walk with Wisdom the more we will walk with wisdom.

"Making the best use of the time" (4:5) means identifying the best times and the best ways of doing good for and to others. Wisdom in how we use our time and what we do with our time will communicate an awareness of God's presence. We can show that there is more to life than time, that there is also an eternity to think about and prepare for.

It's all very well to talk well,
but we must also walk well.

Do I do more than walk with wisdom?

We Talk with Wisdom 4:6

"Let your speech always be gracious" (4:6). It's not enough to say the right thing; we must also say it in the right way. *Gracious* means dealing with people not as they deserve, not as they speak to us. We don't just speak *of* grace but we speak *with* grace.

"Seasoned with salt" (4:6). Salt stops corruption and brings out the flavor of food. Avoid all corrupt talk and bland talk. A wise walk plus wise talk adds seasoning to the gospel feast. Salty speech is appetizing speech.

"So that you may know how you ought to answer each person" (4:6). If we had a formula or script to follow, we wouldn't need prayer. We need prayer because every person and every situation is so unique that we need God's guidance in starting conversations, answering questions, manner, timing, and so on.

If we walk and talk with wisdom,
people will ask for our wisdom.

Changing Our Story with God's Story

Some of us walk the walk but never talk the talk. Some of us talk the talk but don't walk the walk. God's way is a wise walk plus wise talk that maximizes gospel opportunities and gospel success.

Jesus exemplified verses 2–6 perfectly in his life. We worship him as the one who talked to God constantly, and talked to others clearly, courageously, and carefully. As such, he is our example. But he also offers to cover all our failings, wipes out our record, and so motivates us again to follow his model.

Summary: What does a careful witness look like? *Combine a wise walk with wise talk to attract the wise-less to Wisdom.*

Question: Think back to a time when you were careless in witnessing. What would you do differently?

Prayer: Wise Witness, make me a wise witness for you so that I attract people to Jesus rather than repulse them.

Spiritual friendship is a Spirit-friendship.

49

Be a Friend to Have a Friend

COLOSSIANS 4:7–18

Having parented four kids through their teen years, I've seen their hopes of satisfying friendships raised and dashed more times than I can count. Many "best friends forever" became worst friends for nothing.

But I'm not much better myself. My problem is not so much trying to get too many friends, but not even trying to get one friend! Like many men, I act like I'm fine without any close friends. However, although I spare myself the dramas of friendship, I also miss out on the delights of friendship. By distancing myself from what could be painful, I also run from what could be full of pleasure.

Both my teens and myself (and you) need help from the apostle Paul to pursue the right friendships in the right way. In his closing remarks in Colossians 4:7–18, Paul answers the question, *How do we get good friends?*

Christlike Friendship Is Spiritual Friendship 4:7–18

Although Paul's farewell remarks look like a list of irrelevant names and details, it completes the letter about being complete in Christ by showing how spiritual friendship can encourage that completeness.

A spiritual friendship differs from ordinary friendship in that it always involves giving and getting spiritual good such as faith, love, hope, repentance, and grace. Spiritual friendship is a friendship that is founded on spiritual oneness, deepens our spiritual identity, grows in spiritual grace, stimulates spiritual usefulness, and helps us toward our spiritual home.

Spiritual friendship is a Spirit-friendship.

*What kind of people should
I be spiritual friends with?*

Christlike Friendship Is Diverse Friendship 4:7–18

Spiritual friendship is usually more diverse than ordinary friendship, as Paul demonstrates. He didn't limit himself to people just like him, but befriended people from different backgrounds and different social groups, with different interests, gifts, and personalities.

- *He was friends with a range of missionaries:* He mentions Tychicus (4:7), Justus (4:11), and Archippus (4:17), all of whom had different ministries and missions.
- *He was friends with slaves:* Onesimus was a runaway slave. He was on the lowest rung of the social ladder (4:9).
- *He was friends with prisoners:* Aristarchus had been converted through Paul's ministry (Acts 17:1–9), served with him in various places (Acts 19:29; 20:4; 27:2), and was now in prison with him (4:10).
- *He was friends with a failed friend:* Although Paul and Mark had previously fallen out over Mark's defection (Acts 13:13; 15:36–41), God had redeemed this friendship and Mark is now imprisoned together with Paul (4:10).
- *He was friends with Jews and Gentiles:* He lists three Jewish friends (Aristarchus, Mark, and Jesus Justus) and three Gentile friends (Epaphras, Luke, and Demas).
- *He was friends with a doctor:* Paul calls Luke "the beloved physician" (4:14).
- *He was friends with women:* Paul names Nympha and the church in her house (4:15).

We miss out on a lot if our friendships are only with people like us. That's what worldly friendships are like. Spiritual friendship should be different and is improved by difference.

Biblical diversity is strengthening, not threatening.

Changing Our Story with God's Story

I once spoke to a congregation about the importance of racial and economic diversity in the church, but the response from some indicated that they saw this as a threat to the church. Paul would have been dumbfounded at such an attitude.

Jesus has the most diverse friend group of anyone, which gives us all hope that we can be friends with him, no matter who we are, where we've been, or what we've done.

Summary: How do we get good friends? *Make friends with Christ and offer Christlike friendship to others to enjoy Christian friendship in a hostile world.*

Question: How can you increase the spirituality and diversity of your friendships?

Prayer: Lord Jesus, you are my best friend forever. Help me find and give spiritual friendships that exhibit the diversity of your friendships.

If we want to be changed, we must also be challenged.

50

Encouraging and Exhorting

COLOSSIANS 4:7–18

Let's assume that we've asked God to give us spiritual friendships with a diverse range of Christians. What do we do now? What do we do when we're with our spiritual friends? *How do I give and get spiritual good in my spiritual friendships?*

Again, although we may be tempted to skip over Colossians 4:7–18, thinking they are closing personal words that don't apply to us, a closer look will supply two characteristics of all spiritual friendships.

Christlike Friendship Encourages 4:7–18

Our biggest priority in spiritual friendship is encouragement. Look at all the people Paul encourages and how he does it in so many thoughtful ways.

- *He encourages Tychicus:* Mentioned in four other places in Paul's letters, here Paul identifies his special envoy with a special description: a "beloved brother and faithful minister and fellow servant in the Lord" (4:7).
- *He encourages the Colossians:* Paul sent Tychicus "for this very purpose, that you may know how we are and that he may encourage your hearts" (4:8). Paul encourages them by sharing his news through Tychicus.
- *He encourages Onesimus:* He doesn't call Onesimus a slave but "our faithful and beloved brother, who is one of you" (4:9).

- *He encourages through sending greetings:* He sends six people's greetings to the Colossian church. *Greeting* means "embrace." He was sending them hugs.
- *He encourages by recognizing hard work:* Epaphras is singled out for his hard work in prayer for the Colossians (4:12–13).
- *He encourages with love:* He loved the beloved Luke (4:14).
- *He encourages other churches:* "Give my greetings to . . . Nympha and the church in her house" (4:15).
- *He encourages with God's call:* "And say to Archippus, 'See that you fulfill the ministry that you have received in the Lord'" (4:17).
- *He encourages with grace:* He ends where he began—by sending grace (1:2; 4:18).

Paul reveals the encouraging heart of Christ that lies behind these words. Ultimately it's Christ who is encouraging his people.

Christ encourages his people through his encouraging people.

I need encouragement in my friendships,
but I also need to be challenged.

Christlike Friendship Exhorts 4:7–18

Spiritual friendship is not just tender; it's also tough. It spurs others on.

- *He exhorts the Colossians to be personal encouragers:* Although the whole letter is encouraging, these final verses exemplify personally tailored encouragement.
- *He exhorts them to suffer for the gospel:* By mentioning that he is in prison (and he doesn't regret this), he's challenging them to suffer for the gospel (4:10).
- *He exhorts them to faithfulness and love:* He does this by commending these characteristics in Tychicus (4:7), Onesimus (4:9), and Luke (4:14).
- *He exhorts them to welcome visitors:* He called them to warmly receive Mark if he came to them (4:10).

- *He exhorts them to pray:* He highlights Epaphrus's prayer ministry, describing it using the same word for a soldier fighting for his life on the battlefield (4:12).
- *He exhorts them to spiritual maturity and certainty:* Epaphrus was praying that they "may stand mature [complete] and fully assured in all the will of God" (4:12).
- *He exhorts them to labor:* He points to Epaphrus's example of hard work wherever he went (4:13).
- *He exhorts them to persevere in ministry:* He sends a message to Archippus that "you fulfill the ministry that you have received in the Lord" (4:17).
- *He exhorts them to remember his chains* (4:18).

The best friends don't just say what we want to hear but what we need to hear. That's why Paul can be a great friend to us, and Christ can be the best friend to us.

If we want to be changed, we must also be challenged.

Changing Our Story with God's Story

What a friend we have in Jesus! The best friend in the world cannot encourage or exhort like Jesus does.

Summary: How do I give and get spiritual good in my spiritual friendships? *Give and get exhortation and encouragement from Christ and from Christians.*

Question: Have you asked your spiritual friends to encourage and exhort you, to comfort you and challenge you? And do you do that for them?

Prayer: My Best Friend, thank you for encouraging and exhorting me through your people so that I can be complete in Christ.

TheStoryChanger.life

To keep changing your story with God's Story, visit www.thestory changer.life for the latest news about more StoryChanger devotionals, to sign up for the StoryChanger newsletter, and to subscribe to the *The StoryChanger* podcast.